FAMILY
WEALTH
PROTECTION
PLANNING™

James L. Moore

Attorney and Counselor at Law

Publishing-Partners

Publishing-Partners
Port Townsend, WA
books@publishing-partners.com
www.Publishing-Partners.com

Printed in the United States of America

Library of Congress Control Number 2016951277
ISBN: 978-1-944887-08-7
eISBN: 978-1-994887-09-4

The author is not engaged in rendering legal, tax, accounting, or similar professional services. While legal, tax, and accounting issues covered in this book have been checked with sources believed to be reliable, some material may be affected by changes in the laws or in the interpretations of such laws since the manuscript for this book was completed. For that reason the accuracy and completeness of such information and the opinions based thereon are not guaranteed. In addition, state or local laws or procedural rules may have a material impact on the general recommendations made by the author, and the strategies outlined in this book may not be suitable for every individual. If legal, accounting, tax, investment, or other expert advice is required, obtain the services of a competent practitioner.

Table of Contents

DEDICATION

For my incredible wife and life's journey partner, Jan,
who has enabled me to appreciate, in our shared labor
and adventure, the force of St. Augustine's remark that
"a friend is someone with whom one may dare to share
the counsel of one's heart," and without whom I would
not be the man, husband, father and grandfather that
I am and continue to aspire to be. You truly are "my
special angel."

ACKNOWLEDGMENTS

I owe this book to the series of teachers, coaches, friends, fellow U S Marines, and mentors who taught me the truth about success and life. They entered my life at just the right moments to help me with my journey. They helped me plot a course, rebuild after running aground, hitting rocks, or getting lost in the jungle. Present or absent and in some cases deceased, they have been there through the entire journey as steadfast supporters of my dreams. They represent the best of me.

I wish to acknowledge my colleagues and fellow members of the National Network of Estate Planning Attorneys. Their collective expertise, incredible spirit, tremendous energy, and untiring efforts as my "band of brothers" have been immensely helpful to me for many years and are greatly appreciated.

I would also like to acknowledge, as an author, for input on some of the chapters and for the ideas, processes, and techniques described in the book which were created by virtue of my licensing and membership as a Founding Member and Senior Contributing Fellow of the National Network of Estate Planning Attorneys, specifically, Rick Randall, Esq.; Randall Borkus, Esq.; and Bill Liston, Esq.

∼

Thanks to Bob Esperti, Esq. and Reno Peterson, Esq., who created the foundation upon which this latest iteration was written.

~

Thanks to Bruce Raymond Wright, The Wright Company, and to J. David Kerr, Esq., The Kerr Law Firm, for contributing the excellent content in Chapters 12 and 19 respectively.

~

Finally, my incredible, amazing, blended family (children, step-children, grandchildren, great-grandchildren, sons and daughters-in-law). I know of no greater purpose to do anything in life, personally or professionally, than the purpose of helping the next generation stand on our shoulders to make future generations better. Jan and I don't expect you to follow our course; we want you to follow your own courses. Your dreams and your journey are entirely up to you. You decide both the journey and the destination. Just know we'll be there every step of the way, cheering you on and telling you to Go For It! Dream big, work hard, have fun and never, ever give up on your dreams or let anyone steal your dreams. We love you.

FOREWORD

This book addresses a perennial yet modern challenge: we live in times when the more successful you are, the bigger the piece the taxing bodies and even the larger society (via lawsuits) want from you. There is an inherent attempt to redistribute the wealth in our times, which becomes especially true for those who choose to ignore that fact. There are also many misconceptions about how to prepare our heirs and pass on human values, family wealth, and healthy stewardship guidance. We all want those we love to pick up the reins of a family's wealth and values and, hopefully, continue to pass these opportunities on to future generations. But how do we ensure that our loved ones are empowered to do so?

Jamie has broken down the barriers to such family planning challenges and created bite-sized nodules of information that explain what otherwise would be confusing and unachievable. He has done us all a service with his very understandable and readable guidance.

Many professionals have attempted to educate the masses on family wealth protection, but no one I've ever read is as clear as Jamie Moore is in this book. His expertise comes from years and years of experience; he is a true counselor when it comes to family protection challenges, and an artist in the way he explains these complicated concepts. I enjoy the way he puts everything in terms that are comforting to all who have the good fortune to read his book.

I expect that everyone who reads this book cover to cover will walk away with a much better understanding of the questions they should be asking about their family's future. He not only guides the reader through the practical steps of exiting and transitioning a family business, but he also provides a vision for preparing the heirs to pick up the baton.

Dealing with family communications and protecting family wealth and legacy has always been a challenge. One only need to look in the Old Testament to see that it has been part of the human condition for a long time; early biblical writings describe the challenges of families, responsibilities, and wealth transfer. So why is it so hard? Maybe it's just because there hasn't been practical guidance available (since the Bible) until Jamie wrote this book?

Jamie Moore is a true family wealth counselor who has blessed my family as well as many other families with his friendship, mentorship, and down-to-earth practical guidance and user friendly approach to family wealth protection planning. It's an honor to be part of his achievement.

Thanks,

Randall H. Borkus, MS, JD, LL.M./Tax

Borkus Collins Law, PA

Illinois, Florida

www.BorkusCollins.com

INTRODUCTION

Don't be afraid for I am with you. Don't be discouraged for I am your God. I will strengthen you and help you. I will hold you up with my victorious hand.

(Isaiah 41:10)

M y goal is to provide a road map through the complicated and, more often than not, confusing world of estate planning in order to reduce, and in some cases eliminate, people's anxiety and fear about their future.

My second objective is to familiarize you with the Family Wealth Protection Planning™ process; to impart a good understanding of the process, to give you a level of comfort and security that will motivate you to be proactive versus reactive in your planning and act in your own best interest by seeking the assistance of truly collaborative estate, tax, and financial planning professionals.

I do not believe that you should attempt to plan your estate by yourself; estate planning loners generally do not achieve good planning results. A little bit of knowledge can be very dangerous with regard to the FWPP—dangerous if it is viewed as complete or ultimate knowledge. On the other hand, a little bit of knowledge can go a long way if it is used to initiate the selection and monitoring of good professionals to assist you in accomplishing your objectives.

How-to-do-it books may be fun to read, but using fill-in-the-blank estate planning or canned software or the Internet can be worse than doing no planning at all. Good planning necessitates a motivated and knowledgeable client who interacts with professional advisors to bring out the very best in them with respect to their knowledge. In our law firm, it's all about peace of mind, not a piece of paper.

Now, more than ever, knowledge is king. Or, rather, correct, accurate knowledge with appropriate application and implementation is king. That is what I believe this book offers.

PART I

ALIVE AND WELL

1

WHAT IS FAMILY WEALTH PROTECTION PLANNING?

"Show Me the Money"

When a man does not know what harbor he is heading for,
no wind is the right wind.

Seneca

What is Family Wealth Protection Planning™ (FWPP)? It's all the people in your life regardless of their relationship to you. Whether they are related to you by blood, marriage, love, or close friendship, or they are colleagues. It's all about their well-being, prosperity, peace of mind, and security without you.

It is also your professional relationships: lawyers, accountants, insurance people, bankers, and financial planners, coupled with society's rules, laws, taxes, red tape, and the courts who administer and interpret these rules.

It can be a scary, complicated world of all of these advisors trying to accomplish things that most people do not understand involving three separate but important elements: time, human energy and emotion, and money.

FWPP takes time, a little now, or a lot later, to identify and accomplish goals that are personally important to you.

FWPP involves money and finance. It requires dollars, lots of dollars, to both create and maintain your lifestyle for you and your family while you are alive, and after your death. It requires the usage and balancing of your dollars to purchase life insurance or investments based on a desire to create security for your loved ones.

FWPP is alive-and-well planning. It is your desire to use your time, talents, and treasure to create a scenario for yourself and others that will not only be sufficient for you but will extend beyond your life.

FWPP provides an opportunity for you to control your success when you are alive and well, alive and not well, or not alive.

The Truth about Estate Planning is that most plans just don't work, meaning they don't meet client expectations. **A Plan that Works** allows you to meet the definition of estate planning: to maintain control during your lifetime, plan for your disability, then give what you have to whom you want, when you want, and the way that you want.

If asked, you probably know basically what you want to do with your property both during life and after death. You may even be aware of society's rules and the complexity they involve. We believe you need professional help to accomplish your planning goals and objectives.

Everything about you is unique; therefore, your FWPP must also be unique. You must understand the process. Understanding leads to comfort. Planning without understanding results in uncertainty and anxiety. Just like a good pair of pants, one size does not fit all. Our main objective is to help you understand the rules of engagement and take the mystery out of planning; replace it with peace of mind, not a piece of paper.

With a foundation of understanding and the comfort of knowledge, you should be able to confidently put together a terrific team of advisors. You should also be able to communicate your goals to those advisors. When you finish this book you should have a good idea of the FWPP process and also be able to discern between the truly knowledgeable and the not-so-knowledgeable advisor. We believe you will also gain enough understanding of the planning process to empower you to participate in a meaningful dealing with your advisors.

We have all struggled during our lives with procrastination. We understand that "pro" means to be for something. We aren't sure exactly what "crastination" means, but we are against it! As it turns out, the root of the word "crastination" is the Latin term *crastinus*, which means to postpone something continually. So procrastination means to put something off forever, not just until tomorrow.

Without FWPP, tomorrow may instantly become today. None of us can accurately predict the exact date of our disability or death. Disability and death, and their timing, are no respecters of persons. Tomorrow Land only exists in fairy tales. Now is the best time to plan—not later.

Fortunately, FWPP™ only begins when you are alive and well. It can continue through disability, death, and even after death.

As you will learn from some of the stories and examples in this book, we often hear, "FWPP for me? Really? Hey, dude, we aren't Jed Clampett or Bill Gates." The truth is that FWPP is an American process for all Americans. Fortunately, it is not unique to any economic or social class.

We all hear, "I really don't need FWPP. We only have a few acorns anyway."

Really? No loved ones, no favorite family members, no close friends or institutions, no partner, no property, no insurance, no pension plan, no personal property or family heirlooms, no dreams, goals, aspirations, or fears?

FWPP is for virtually everyone and it is getting more complex every day. Congress continues to pass new tax and other laws. Each time the laws become more complicated and affect more people. We believe that in many ways a lot of taxes are voluntary. People with knowledge of and access to expert professionals can escape most of these taxes.

That is why we call it FWPP. It now involves many different disciplines, tools, and techniques, and, of course, an expanded and changing meaning of the term "family."

This book is designed to help you wade through the swamp without getting eaten by the alligators. We believe as you read this book you will begin thinking about the incredible opportunities there are for planning and not the obstacles that may get in the way.

The reason we exist and continue to do this work is to help

people reduce and, in some cases, eliminate the fear and anxiety that is created without any planning and replace it with peace of mind. We believe now is the time for you to plan for, protect, and preserve your wealth and values because, in our experience, we have learned that the major problem is that most "traditional" estate plans just don't work!

We know an estate plan works when the expectations of the client are completely met. Of course, it's really the family members who see the results. Why don't most plans work? We believe it's because many clients and professional advisors see estate planning as being transactional. They say, "I did my estate plan." **In reality, estate planning is a process, not a transaction.** Because everything constantly changes, your plan must be changing too.

2

PROTECTING YOUR ACORNS FROM THE BAD GUYS

Creditors and Predators and Lawsuits—Oh My!

Obstacles are like wild animals. They are cowards but they will bluff you if they can. If they see you are afraid of them...they are liable to spring upon you; but...if you look them squarely in the eye, they will slink out of sight.

Orison Swett Marden

One of the common interpretations of the concept of asset protection is that an individual, family, or business is trying to avoid paying well-deserved creditors. That is not the purpose of asset protection.

We live in a litigious society. It is common for unhappy people to attempt to solve their problems by resorting to a lawsuit. Creative attorneys and receptive courts have had the effect of broadening the reach of litigation. As a result, huge judgments are awarded in cases that one would not expect to even go to court.

The purpose of asset protection is to title assets in such a manner as to discourage lawsuits that are unreasonable in their scope, as well as avoid the horrendous monetary demands of plaintiffs. Short of discouraging the lawsuit itself, asset protection encourages plaintiffs to settle their claims on a more reasonable basis because of the difficulties they encounter in collecting from the defendant.

There are numerous asset protection techniques. This chapter deals with the best-known methods.

Insurance

A great deal of the liability risks most of us face can be insured against. One of the first steps in asset protection is to meet with your liability insurance carrier to assess your assets and your lifestyle to determine your need for basic liability coverage and amplified umbrella insurance. Find out what the coverage costs and what it covers. You are then better able to determine whether asset protection is necessary and whether the cost of insurance is such that other forms of asset protection are warranted.

Holding Property in Tenancy by the Entirety

An inexpensive and relatively effective method of asset protection for married couples is to hold title to marital property as *tenants by the entirety*. Michigan allows tenants by the entirety ownership, which means that neither a creditor of only the husband nor a creditor of only the wife can get a judgment against tenancy by the entirety property. For example, let's say that John is an executive with a large company and his wife, Terri, is a physician. John's exposure to litigation may be small, but Terri's could be very high. If all of John and Terri's property were not held in tenancy by the entirety, a patient could sue Terri for millions and win a judgment for an amount far greater than her malpractice coverage. But even though there is a judgment, the patient could not take John and Terri's assets if they were held in tenancy by the entirety.

However, if John and Terri were to divorce and split the property, Terri's separate assets would then be subject to the judgment. Also, if John were to die while the judgment was outstanding, then all the assets would pass to Terri by law. At that point, they would be subject to the claims of her creditors.

The more likely outcome is that when the patient's lawyers find out that Terri is judgment-proof because of the way her property is titled, they will want to settle the case. It is also likely that the settlement will be within Terri's malpractice insurance limits. Settling within these limits is a clear victory for Terri and John; it allows them to preserve their assets while paying for the consequences of Dr. Terri's actions.

Investing in Exempt Assets

One simple method of asset protection is to invest in assets that are free from the claims of creditors by either state or federal law. While state law provides for more exempt assets than does federal law, each can be taken advantage of for purposes of asset protection.

The primary exempt asset under federal law is a qualified retirement plan such as a profit sharing plan, a money purchase pension plan, or a defined benefit pension plan. Assets in these plans, by law, cannot be taken by creditors of the plan participant. However, plans that are not considered to be qualified, such as Individual Retirement Accounts (IRAs), are not protected under federal law. A majority of the states do protect IRAs and other nonqualified retirement plans from creditors. Michigan law provides for a partial protection for IRAs. Michigan also provides a homestead exemption. The objective of a homestead exemption is to protect a person's primary residence from being taken by creditors.

Life insurance proceeds paid to named beneficiaries are generally protected from claims of creditors of the insured. Sometimes the proceeds are also protected from creditors of the beneficiary. In addition, Michigan protects the cash value of life insurance, when the policy is owned by the insured. The value of an annuity and the proceeds from an annuity may also be protected from creditors of the annuitant.

Finally, most states have some minor exemptions for personal property. However, none of these exemptions are very large and they should not be relied upon as any sort of comprehensive asset protection planning.

Using a Corporation or Limited Liability Company to Protect Assets

One of the primary reasons that businesses incorporate or form a limited liability company (LLC) is for the asset protection of their shareholders or members. If a corporation or LLC is sued or goes bankrupt, the members or shareholders generally can lose only the value of their stock or membership interest. Theoretically, they are not personally liable. We say "theoretically" because if a shareholder or member takes some action that is deemed fraudulent or in violation of the articles, the shareholder or member could be liable for some or all of the corporate debts. In the case of closely held businesses (those with very few shareholders or members who are also involved in the corporation's business operations), it is very possible that in any lawsuit against the corporation or LLC the shareholders or members will be sued also.

Corporations and LLCs are often used for limited asset protection. When they are used, it is to isolate particular assets. For example, let's say that Harvey owns a fireworks company. If the entire operation blows up, Harvey would not like to lose his other assets. Harvey would be wise to incorporate his business or form an LLC. Now, Harvey could still be sued, but if he has kept his business entity up by paying annual fees, filing annual reports, making sure the public is aware that it is dealing with an entity, not Harvey, and meeting all other state requirements, odds are that Harvey has protected his other assets.

A corporation or LLC can protect an owner's other assets, but only if the business entity is clearly separate and apart from its owners. This does not mean the owners cannot work in the business, but it does mean that the owners must observe all formalities of the business. If Harvey does work in the business and he is the person who negligently packed the fireworks that exploded, then he can be sued for his personal negligence.

A corporation or LLC does not protect an owner, an officer, or an employee from his or her own acts. That is why a corporation or LLC may not be the best asset protection in the world for an individual who wants to protect more than his or her investment in a business.

One of the problems of using a corporate or LLC structure without other asset protection planning is the application of Murphy's Law: "What can go wrong, will go wrong." If Harvey gets into an automobile accident and is sued for millions of dollars over and above his insurance coverage, then he may lose his corporate stock or LLC memberships as well as the remainder of his assets. In asset protection, it is not always the obvious liability that comes back to haunt you. It is just as likely that some unexpected action will cause the need for asset protection.

Limited Partnerships

A limited partnership is a business structure that has two types of owners. The general partner is in charge of the management of the partnership, and has unlimited liability. The other owners are called limited partners. Much like shareholders in a corporation, they do not have any liability other than the value of their limited partnership interests. Limited partners are not allowed to participate in the management of the partnership; if they do, then they lose their liability protection.

Well-structured limited partnership agreements provide that the general partners and the limited partners cannot sell, give, or in any manner dispose of their interests in the limited partnership without the consent of all the other partners. This provision works well in the asset protection arena. If a creditor has a judgment against a partner, that creditor cannot be a legitimate owner. Therefore, the creditor has no standing to "step in the shoes" of the partner who owes the creditor. This provision makes the partnership interests unattractive for creditors.

The best a creditor can hope for is to go to court and obtain a legal document called a charging order. A charging order allows the creditor to seize any distributions from the partnership that would otherwise go to the partner who owes the judgment to the creditor.

If the limited partnership is comprised of family members or related parties, as in asset protection limited partnerships, then it is unlikely a distribution will be forthcoming. Thus the creditor may have to wait a long time to collect the amount of the judgment. This encourages the creditor to settle rather than wait.

A charging order does cause a very serious potential problem for the creditor. The Internal Revenue Service takes the position that a creditor holding a charging order is responsible for the partner's share of taxable income. Let's say that a limited partnership has $100,000 of taxable income, but the general partner decides not to distribute any cash. The partners are still responsible for their share of the partnership's taxes. If Limited Partner A owns 25 percent of the partnership, but A's creditor has a charging order, the creditor must include 25 percent of the partnership's taxable income on the creditor's income tax return, even if the creditor has not been paid a dime! This feature discourages some creditors from seeking a charging order; again, it is a method to help settle the debt with the creditor.

One of the weaknesses of a limited partnership is that the general partner is liable for all partnership debts and liabilities. Often, a general partnership is held in a business entity, such as a corporation or a limited liability company, to reduce the exposure of the individual who would otherwise be the general partner.

Another potential weakness of a limited partnership is that a court may find that the partnership is a sham and should be ignored for purposes of a judgment. Courts do this if the partnership is not properly formed, not properly funded, or not properly operated, or is clearly set up solely for purposes of defrauding creditors. For these reasons, it is imperative that an individual or family consult with an attorney who is an expert in asset protection planning before setting up a limited partnership. These are complex business organizations that need the attention of a professional.

More About Limited Liability Companies

A limited liability company is a hybrid between a corporation and a limited partnership. Like a corporation, all of a limited liability company's owners are protected from the debts and liabilities of the company. Like a partnership, a limited liability company does not have its own tax liability; income and losses are passed through to the owners, based on their percentage of ownership.

Limited liability companies are popular for several reasons. The primary reason for their popularity is that the owners of a limited liability company can participate in management. Contrast this participation to that of a limited partnership; in order to maintain limited liability, the limited partners cannot participate in management.

Another reason for the popularity of limited liability companies is that they are taxed like an S corporation or a partnership. Limited liability companies do not have a separate tax liability, so all income, deductions, and credits are passed through to the owners based on their ownership percentages. Unlike an S corporation, which is subject to a number of rules respecting who can and cannot be owners, practically any person or entity can own a limited liability company.

Just as in corporations, however, limited liability companies offer only limited asset protection. They protect the owners from losing more than their investment, assuming all the required limited liability formalities are met, but do not necessarily prevent a creditor from taking the ownership interest itself. The remedy of a charging order for a limited liability company is not necessarily available, so absent state legislation to the contrary, limited liability companies are not used for overall asset protection.

Michigan law recognizes the concept of "spendthrift provisions." This is an essential component of even a revocable trust. Here is why: Suppose you create a revocable living trust that provides, among other things, that upon your death some of your assets will pass to an irrevocable subtrust for the benefit of your children. You allow the trustee to make the decision as to whether or when income and principal will be paid out to your children. You also allow the trustee to pay out trust income and principal on behalf of a child. That means that instead of giving money directly to the child for rent, for example, the trustee pays the rent directly. The trust also includes a spendthrift provision.

After your death, one of your children has creditor or predator problems. Creditors will seize any money he or she receives directly. However, if the trustee makes payments on behalf of your child, then the creditors cannot seize either the money paid or the trust assets.

As you can see, spendthrift planning is important in trusts for the beneficiaries. That is one reason why you should work with a highly skilled estate planning attorney and other advisors so that these issues can be addressed properly.

Offshore Asset Protection Trusts

The most sophisticated method for asset protection is the offshore asset protection trust (OAPT). These trusts have become quite popular over the last decade and have proven to be effective in asset protection, despite critical articles to the contrary.

In a nutshell, an OAPT is an irrevocable trust that is set up in a country outside of the United States. A number of countries can be used, but some of the most popular are the Isle of Man, the Cook Islands, and the Cayman Islands. Even though the trust is irrevocable, it provides provisions that in essence allow the maker to have the benefit of the assets. There are build-in mechanisms that allow the maker to retrieve the assets if he or she needs them.

Unlike a domestic irrevocable trust, OAPTs require that creditors bring their lawsuits in the foreign country rather than the United States. The countries that are used for the situs of an OAPT do not recognize United States judgments. So, for example, if a creditor has a court order to seize the assets of a United States person who has his or her property in an OAPT, the creditor cannot go to a court in the foreign jurisdiction and ask the courts there to enforce it. The courts in the foreign jurisdiction will require a full trial there in order to determine the validity of the claim.

Even if the claim is valid, the foreign jurisdictions do not allow creditors of the trustmaker to take trust assets unless the creditor can prove that the assets were fraudulently conveyed to the trust. Typically, these countries make proving fraudulent conveyances very difficult. In addition, they have relatively short statutes of limitation for bringing a fraudulent conveyance action; it is highly likely that the statute of limitations will expire prior to the time that the creditor comes to the foreign country.

Because of the way OAPTs are drafted, the maker of the trust does not lose a great deal of control over his or her assets. Most practitioners who draft these trusts start with a domestic family limited partnership that owns all, or substantially all, of the maker's assets. The maker then transfers his or her assets to the partnership in exchange for the general and limited partnership assets. The limited partnership interests are transferred to the OAPT. The maker controls the assets in the partnership because he or she is the general partner.

The limited partnership allows the maker to invest assets freely, with few restrictions. However, at the first sign of litigation, the maker can liquidate the assets in the partnership and transfer the proceeds into the OAPT. The liquidation and transfer get the assets out of the reach of United States courts.

OAPTs are not as effective for real estate as they are for other types of property such as stocks, bonds, and investment accounts. The latter assets are movable; real estate is not. Because real estate is not movable, a United States court can seize it even if the property is technically owned by an OAPT.

One common fear of people thinking about creating an OAPT is that they will get into trouble with a court and a judge may send them to jail if they do not take assets out of their trust. A unique feature of an offshore trust that is created in a proper jurisdiction is that the foreign jurisdiction's laws will prohibit the trustee from paying the assets to a maker who is under duress. So, if a court orders the maker to force the foreign trustee to give the assets back, the maker can agree to do so. But the trustee cannot comply under the laws of the foreign jurisdiction. The trustee can only pay over assets if the maker requests that the trustee do so and if the maker is not being forced to make the request.

Do not ever attempt to set up an OAPT by yourself or with someone who does not have absolutely impeccable credentials in offshore asset protection planning. These are complex trusts that require precision in their drafting and implementation. Generally speaking, OAPTs fail because they are not drafted correctly or they are incorrectly funded. Handled with expertise, they are very effective in motivating creditors to settle on a reasonable basis.

Fraudulent Conveyances

All states in the United States and most foreign jurisdictions make it unlawful to make a conveyance that is designed to hinder, delay, or defraud an existing creditor or a creditor who is known and could have a basis for a valid claim. That type of transfer is a fraudulent conveyance, and the recipient of the conveyance must return the asset.

Michigan has a broad fraudulent conveyance statute. Prior to entering into any asset protection planning, you must consult with an attorney who will give you guidance about this statute, as well as others that may apply. Please understand that asset protection should be accomplished prior to encountering a problem, not afterward. If you have a creditor problem now, or think that you may, asset protection planning may not be for you. An attorney or other advisor who helps you make such a conveyance can get in a lot of trouble, as you can.

It is in the area of fraudulent conveyances that OAPTs are commonly, and correctly, criticized as being immoral, potentially ineffective, and crooked. However, if they are created innocently before a cause of action arises, none of these labels can attach.

Asset protection planning, even at its base level, is no area for rookies or do-it-yourselfers. Use a team of professionals if you want asset protection to be a part of your estate planning.

3

TRUSTS

The Estate Planner's Toolbox

No one was ever lost on a straight road.

Proverb From India

S everal, if not all, estate planning techniques can be implemented in the form of a trust, including a host of trust and various ancillary documents, in order to accomplish the planning objectives of our clients. An Estate Planner uses trusts like an experienced professional mechanic or master carpenter uses a tool box. The subject of trusts and how they are used is seldom taught outside of the various professional disciplines of law, accounting, and financial planning. In our experience, however, very few clients we initially meet understand what trusts do, what they involve, and how they are structured.

In estate planning, trusts enable people to pass title to their property to others either during lifetime or at death. When a person creates a trust and places property in a trust, the trustmaker, in effect, makes a gift. Trusts enable their makers to make gifts to their beneficiaries and allow the trustmaker to exercise significant control, on a prearranged basis, over the disposition of the trust property. In effect, trusts allow property to pass to others with strings attached.

All trusts have the following characteristics:

- A trust is created by a trustmaker.

- Some attorneys call the maker a settlor, trustor, creator, or grantor.

- The person responsible for following the maker's instructions is called the trustee.

- Trustees can be individuals or licensed institutions. The maker can also be his or her own trustee.

- Trusts can be created by more than one maker. Joint makers are called joint makers or comakers. Trusts can be operated by more than one trustee, called cotrustees.

- Trusts can be created for the benefit of the maker or for the benefit of other people. The people for whose benefit a trust is created are called beneficiaries.

- Trusts can accomplish just about any objective of the maker as long as it is not illegal or against public policy.

- Trusts cannot last forever unless the beneficiary is a legally recognized charity or unless state law allows them to last forever.

- The beneficiaries who have the first rights to the trust property are called primary beneficiaries. If the primary beneficiaries die or become disqualified, and according to the instructions given to the trustee by the trustmaker, then the property will go to other named beneficiaries called contingent beneficiaries.

- Trusts, to be effective, must be in writing. They must be signed by the maker, and if a living trust is used, it should be signed by the trustee.

- The law has always stated that "No trust shall fail for lack of a trustee." The local court having jurisdiction over trusts will name a trustee if one is not named in the trust document.

- Trust beneficiaries do not have to sign the trust document or will containing a trust.

- Any number of separate trusts can be created in a single trust document.

- When the maker puts property in a trust, the maker funds the trust.

- Trustmakers can be primary or contingent beneficiaries of their own trusts.

There are several different kinds of trusts that accomplish a host of estate planning objectives. (Please refer to Figure 3-1.) All trusts can be categorized in one of two ways. A trust is either a living trust or a death trust. Living trusts are often referred to as *inter vivos* (Latin for living) trusts. Death trusts are called testamentary (from the Latin *testamentum*) trusts and are created in a person's will. They do not come into existence until the death of the will maker.

A living trust is always created during the lifetime of the trustmaker. A living trust usually provides that the maker is to be his or her own primary beneficiary. Living trusts can also pass the trust property to the maker's beneficiaries on the maker's death. Because living trusts can pass property on the death of the maker, they are often referred to as will substitutes.

A death, or testamentary, trust can only be created in a valid will. These trusts are never created to benefit the maker. Death trusts are created by a will maker, and although they are created or drafted during the will maker's life, they are not operative until the maker's death. Death trusts have no life until the death of the maker.

Because a will goes through the probate process, the trusts created in that will also go through the probate process. Testamentary trusts are involved in the probate process and are subject to the local probate court's direction and control (jurisdiction).

Testamentary Trusts

A will with a trust inside of it
- ▶ not effective until death
- ▶ must go through probate

Inter Vivos Trusts

Living Trusts

Created during lifetime
- ▶ will substitute
- ▶ avoids probate

Revocable Living Trust

- ▶ changeable during lifetime
- ▶ trustmaker keeps total control
- ▶ can include disability planning
- ▶ generally does not involve gifts

Irrevocable Living Trusts

- ▶ cannot be changed
- ▶ "gift" with strings attached
- ▶ trustmaker cannot directly control

Special Irrevocable Trusts

Irrevocable Living Trust

- ▶ involves taxable gifts that qualify for annual exclusion
- ▶ minor has right to property at 21
- ▶ income taxed to minor

Irrevocable Life Insurance Trust

- ▶ involves taxable gifts that qualify for annual exclusion
- ▶ insurance accessible to beneficiaries
- ▶ keeps life insurance federal estate tax -free

Figure 3-1 - Different Kinds of Trusts

Both living trusts and death trusts are important tools to estate planning professionals. They allow professionals to accomplish their clients' estate planning objectives. Estate planning involves more than outright passing of property from one person to another. People want to give what they have, to whom they want, in the way and at the time they want. They wish to reduce taxes, attorney's fees, and court costs to the greatest extent possible, and also to pass along their wisdom with their wealth, if possible. These objectives are almost always accomplished by using various trust formats. Remember that trusts are gifts with strings attached: instructions and conditions given to the trustee as to the who, how and when of distribution of property.

Death trusts can always be canceled or changed by the maker, as long as the maker is competent, up until the maker's death.

Living trusts can be structured so that the maker can retain the right to change or terminate the trust while the maker is alive. Living trusts that give the maker the right to change his or her mind are called revocable living trusts. Living trusts that cannot be changed are called irrevocable living trusts. Neither the maker nor anyone else, for that matter, may alter these trusts.

When a trustmaker creates a revocable living trust, a gift is not made. Because the maker has the right to change his or her mind about the terms of the trust document, there can be no gift for federal gift tax purposes. If, however, property does pass to others while the maker is alive (even if the trust is revocable), there may be a gift for federal gift tax purposes.

It is important to remember that whether a person gives property directly to others or gives property to others through a trust, a gift will always result. Whether that gift will be taxed depends upon the amount of the gift and the circumstances surrounding how the gift was made.

When a trustmaker creates an irrevocable living trust, a gift will always result. By creating an irrevocable trust, a trustmaker gives up all control to the trust property and to the terms of the trust. Once the irrevocable trust is signed, a maker cannot change his or her mind or alter the terms of the trust.

By creating an irrevocable living trust, a trustmaker makes a gift with strings attached. That is usually why these trusts are used. Irrevocable living trusts allow a person to give the use of property to others on a living basis pursuant to the maker's wishes and instructions to the trustee as to its use. Without the use of such a vehicle, gifts could not be made with instructions that would guarantee and control their use. Without the use of an irrevocable trust, a gift made is a gift completed; the recipient can do anything with the property received.

Irrevocable trusts are used in many situations, including:

1. To own life insurance policies on the life of the trustmaker. These trusts are designed to keep the insurance proceeds federal estate tax-free on death.

2. To hold title to property given to minors so that the gift maker can exercise control over the property.

There are many different kinds of trusts that professional estate planners use to accomplish the objectives of their clients. Estate-planning trusts are designed to allow people to pass title to their property to others either during lifetime or at death. In the chapters that follow, we demonstrate how some of these trusts can be utilized to meet most estate planning goals. (Please refer to Appendix B: A Guide to Picking the Right Trust.)

4

REVOCABLE LIVING TRUSTS

The Foundation of Family Wealth Protection Planning™

There are many truths of which the full meaning cannot be realized until personal experience has brought it home.

John Stuart Mill

As the public has become more aware of the often unnecessary costs and time delays associated with wills and probate, many lawyers and other advisors have come to realize that living trusts are in every way superior to will-based planning.

Even Congress, through the Internal Revenue Code, recognizes living trusts as a tremendous force in estate planning.

"To my loyal estate planning attorney, I
leave my children a complicated series of
trusts that will generate huge legal fees."

I have always, in my professional career, strongly believed that estate planning professionals should use the revocable living trust as the main or foundation document to accomplish the majority of their clients' estate planning objectives. The revocable living trust is a most attractive estate planning device. It can be used instead of a will to accomplish the bulk of your estate planning goals. Revocable living trusts have been used successfully for centuries.

In my opinion and that of virtually all my colleagues, they should be used by just about everybody.

Here is an overview of the benefits that can be derived from the use of this amazing estate planning "tool" in the hands of a "master carpenter."

- Provides one planning document full of instructions for your care and the care of your loved ones.

- Provides continuity in the handling of your affairs by efficiently transferring your property to your loved ones.

- Fully avoids probate on your disability or death with respect to its assets.

- Easily moves with you from state to state.

- Creates protective trusts for your loved ones that are free from the supervision of the probate court.

- Can be easily changed should you desire to do so.

- Enables you to rely on your Trustees should you wish to travel or otherwise delegate the day-to-day management of your financial affairs.

- Is difficult for disgruntled heirs to attack.

- Ensures your family's privacy following your disability or death.

- Achieves your death tax objectives.

If you choose to use a revocable living trust you can take advantage of all these benefits. A detailed discussion of each of these benefits follows.

Property Distribution after Your Death

On and after your death, all property in your trust and the income that property generates will be distributed by the trustee according to your precise written instructions.

Property in a revocable living trust can be left to the beneficiaries outright on your death, or it can remain in trust and be distributed over a certain period of time to your beneficiaries. Several trusts can be created within a revocable living trust, which will become operative for designated beneficiaries on your death. In fact, there is no limit to the number of separate trusts that can be created in a single revocable living trust. Each trust that is created within the trust document can spell out its individual terms with regard to the amounts to be distributed and the timing under which those amounts are to pass to your beneficiaries. Each of the trusts created in the trust document may have different terms and conditions as to the distribution of income and principal to your selected beneficiaries.

If you are married, you and your spouse or domestic partner can create a joint revocable living trust. In this single trust for the two of you, you can make all the distributions that each of you want. By creating subtrusts, there are unlimited possibilities for making after-death distributions.

One Receptacle to Receive and Distribute All Property

Through the use of a revocable living trust, you can control the distribution of all your property. This is a trust not only for the property you put in your trust while alive, but also for other property that flows into your trust on your death. Proceeds from life insurance can be left to your trust if you name your trust as the beneficiary; the same is true with respect to proceeds from pension and profit sharing plans. For that matter, any proceeds from third-party beneficiary contracts can be left to your trust if you simply make the trust the beneficiary of those contracts.

Property that is not placed in the trust during your lifetime can still be put in the trust after your death through the use of a short, well-drafted will that attorneys call a *pour-over will*. The provisions of a pour-over will simply state that any property you neglected to put in your trust will, nevertheless, pass to your trust (pour over to it) after your death. The pour-over will should always be used in conjunction with a revocable living trust.

It is important to understand, however, that property owned jointly cannot be put into a trust on your death. Beware of owning jointly held property; you cannot control it on your death, and it may go to unintended heirs.

Take Care of Yourself Too

A revocable living trust can be designed so that it can provide for your care during your lifetime. In your revocable living trust, you can spell out in as much detail as you like how you wish to be taken care of with *your own* trust property in case of your incapacity, which could result from senility, accident, or illness. You can specify who your trustees will be if you become incompetent. You can also provide for the care of your loved ones should you lose control of your mental faculties.

The ability to provide for your care as well as the care of your loved ones during your lifetime is one of the greatest attributes of a revocable living trust.

A revocable living trust can avoid all the confusion and publicity occasioned by court proceedings that would otherwise come about upon your incapacity. This point takes on even greater significance in light of the ability of modern medicine to keep people alive under almost unbelievable circumstances.

All fifty states and the District of Columbia allow the use of a *durable special power of attorney*. This document allows you to give the right to someone you trust to place your property in your revocable living trust if you are unable to do so. It is durable in that, unlike general powers of attorney, its legality continues even if you are incompetent. By using a durable power of attorney as an addition to your revocable living trust, you can assure yourself that your property will be placed in your trust and used pursuant to your directions for you and your loved ones' benefit without costly court interference and publicity.

Private Documents

Unlike a will, revocable living trusts are private documents. They are not made public either while you are alive, at your death, or subsequent to your death. By using a revocable living trust, you can be assured that you will not be taking your affairs and your family's affairs public.

Some professionals take the position from time to time that living trusts are not private because third parties such as banks and financial brokerage firms ask to see the full trust. The reason that they want to see the trust is to make sure that the corrected trustees have the authority to act and that the trust is in effect. However, there is usually no reason for anyone to see the full trust, especially those private provisions as to how you leave your property.

The only parts of a trust that have to be disclosed are the provisions relating to who the trustees are, the powers given to the trustees under the trust document, and evidence that the trust is in existence. Generally, all of this information can be put into a Certificate of Trust, which is then signed by the trustees. Before you disclose anything, consult your attorney to find out what you do need to let others see and what you do not.

Revocable living trusts, their provisions, and the property they control remain the exclusive business of the beneficiaries for whom they were created; other than the trustee, the trusts are nobody else's business.

Easy to Create and Maintain

Revocable living trusts are easy to create. In my opinion, you should always seek out an attorney who knows estate planning, convey your wishes, and set a time for a future meeting to review your trust.

I do not believe that you should fill in preprinted forms sold in books or on the internet. I believe very strongly that you should be knowledgeable but that you should always seek the assistance of estate planning professionals.

Once the attorney completes your plan, sign it if it meets your objectives. That is all there is to it. Unlike a will, the formalities of signing a trust are almost nonexistent. Of course, the trust should be funded. That, too, is not difficult and is discussed at length in Chapter 5.

After creating your revocable living trust, you should check back with your attorney from time to time to make sure your trust has kept current with your objective and with new legal developments. Keeping current is important and can be accomplished through the use of a revocable living trust.

It is a good idea to set a schedule with your attorney and other advisors to periodically review your living trust and your estate and financial planning. In our complex world, changes seem to occur more frequently than ever. By forming a team of trusted advisors and periodically meeting with them, you can exchange ideas and make changes so that your planning will maintain its relevance and stay technically on the cutting edge of planning.

Can be Changed without Formality

Wills have to be signed and executed with a great deal of legal formality, and codicils (will amendments) have the same formal requirements. This is not the case with revocable living trusts. These trusts need only your signature to infuse life into them. Similarly, trust amendments, regardless of their scope, require only your signature.

Avoid Adverse Lifetime Income Tax Consequences

There are no adverse income tax consequences associated with the use of a revocable living trust during your life. Because the trust is revocable, the income generated by the property that is in the name of the trust is taxed to you and is reported on your personal income tax returns. A revocable living trust for which you are the trustee is not required to have a separate federal identification number or file a separate tax return. If you are married, as long as either you or your spouse or domestic partner is a trustee, a separate identification number or tax return is not required. Thus, income generated by the property that is in the name of the revocable living trust requires little extra effort by its maker.

Probate-Free

Property that is in a revocable living trust will not, on your death, go through the probate process. Probate is a process that passes title to assets. Because the title to your property is already in your trust and the trust does not die with you, there is no passing of title required; title has already passed during your life. The probate process is not applicable to trust property.

Total avoidance of probate is an enormous benefit to you and your beneficiaries. It represents significant savings in costs, time, and court interference with respect to your affairs. Funded revocable living trusts avoid the probate process.

Please understand that there are still some administrative expenses for most trusts upon the death of their maker. These fees are substantially less that the standard fees charged for probate and administration.

Continuity in the Handling of Your Affairs

Because there is no probate associated with revocable living trust property, you can be assured that a smooth and uneventful transition will occur with respect to your affairs on your death. Your beneficiaries automatically begin to receive income and principal on your death, pursuant to the terms written in your trust document. This fluidity with regard to your affairs is of major importance because it reduces cost and does not create unnecessary change or crisis for your survivors.

Death Tax Planning Opportunities

A host of techniques are used to reduce federal estate taxes by professional estate planners. Remember, every technique of federal estate tax savings that can be implemented in a will can also be implemented in a revocable living trust.

Good in Every State

Every state's laws recognize the validity of a revocable living trust. A truly beneficial feature attributed to these estate planning documents is that they can cross state lines with their makers without any need to redraft their terms to comply with local law.

You may change your domicile; many people do. We move around the country with increasing regularity. Our moves are usually associated with career opportunities or a better place to live after retirement. With each move the question is generally asked, "Do I have to redo my estate plan?" If a revocable living trust has been used, the answer is no. The state law under which that trust was prepared will still be the law that is used with respect to its legal validity. Most well-written revocable living trusts provide that the law with respect to the administration of the trust will be the law of the state in which the maker and trust reside from time to time.

Revocable living trusts can cross state lines much more easily than their will counterparts. This flexibility gives you the security and knowledge that you will not have to redo your estate plan every time you are transferred or move to another state. Any time you do move to another state, however, you should have your estate plan reviewed by an estate planner in that state, because additional planning opportunities may be available to you with regard to your new state's law. Remember, each state has its own system with respect to death taxes.

Can Measure Trustees during Life

Most trustmakers elect to be their own trustees during their lives. Many of our clients elect to be their own trustees and name their spouse or domestic partners or close family members or friends as cotrustees. The advantage of the cotrusteeship is that on the incapacity or death of the trustmaker, the cotrustee can continue the operation of the trust without the need to seek court assistance.

You may elect, however, to name the persons or professional institutions who will be handling your trust after your death on a current, or living, basis. If you decide to name your death trustees on a current basis, you will be able to observe their performance and abilities as they manage the trust property for your benefit. By using a revocable living trust, you are able to measure the performance of your after-death trustees while you are alive.

Difficult for Disgruntled Heirs to Attack

Most of you are aware of the horror stories associated with unhappy heirs attacking the will of a maker who did not leave those unhappy folks what they thought they had coming. Attorneys call attacking a will *contest*. Will contests occur all too frequently. Wills are usually contested by family members who were cut out or who received less than their anticipated share of the maker's property.

Revocable living trusts are much more difficult for disgruntled heirs to attack than are their will counterparts. Revocable living trusts are private documents that are not involved in the probate process. They are not placed in a public forum that encourages debate and advocacy, as are their will counterparts. They are not subject to all the legal formalities that are associated with wills. Because there are fewer legal rules with regard to their creation, there are fewer legal opportunities to invalidate them. Our experience has driven this point home most convincingly. Our firm has prepared several hundred revocable living trusts over the years, and to the best of our knowledge, not one has ever been attacked, much less attacked successfully.

Criticisms of Revocable Living Trusts

The revocable living trust has so many attractive features unique to it that we cannot understand why it is not used more frequently as a will substitute by more professionals. Many professionals are suspicious of it because they do not understand it. Other professionals are critical of it and allege the following negatives with regard to its use:

- It is difficult to establish and maintain.

- It is expensive.

- It is less effective in limiting creditors' claims after death.

- Gifts from a trust may still be included in the maker's estate for federal estate tax purposes.

- Significant savings on after-death income tax are lost because of its use.

On the contrary, in our experience revocable living trusts are not difficult to establish. A professional estate planner can create them, at times, more easily than their will counterparts.

And in our experience, they are not difficult to maintain. It is true that if you do create a revocable living trust, you will have to take time to organize your affairs and keep them organized within your trust's parameters. We believe that this is a positive feature that should encourage their use. Remember, what you do not do while alive, the probate court and your beneficiaries must do after you are gone. Please read Chapter 18 if you doubt our conclusion.

It is true that revocable living trusts can cost more to create than their will counterparts. The increase in cost is due to an increase in work that is required of the planning professionals. However, drawing up the will is only a small part of the total estate planning job. The attorney will finish the job when the will is taken through the probate process.

Common sense and our experience would indicate a huge difference in cost between wills and fully funded revocable living trusts. Generally, the fee for a will coupled with the cost of probate is enormous when compared to the cost of preparing and funding a revocable living trust.

The attorney who utilizes a revocable living trust as an estate planning vehicle charges one fee. That fee may be for both drafting the document and funding the document so that there will be no probate process. Some attorneys charge separately for funding and some work with other advisors who assume the responsibility of funding the trust.

Some attorneys believe that a revocable living trust is not as effective as a will in cutting off the claims of creditors against the assets of a deceased trustmaker. In all but a few states, however, a revocable living trust is actually a better tool than a will for limiting the claws of both creditors and predators after a trustmaker's death.

Summary of Benefits of Revocable Living Trusts:

- Distribute property after your death.
- Create one receptacle for all your property.
- Take care of yourself, too.
- Offer privacy.
- Easy to create and maintain.
- Easily changed.
- No adverse lifetime or after-death income tax consequences.
- Probate-free.
- Continuity in your affairs.
- Planning for death tax.
- Good in every state.
- Can measure trustees during your life.
- Difficult to attack.

5

FUNDING A REVOCABLE LIVING TRUST

Putting All Your Acorns Into One Bucket

What is, is; and what ain't, ain't.

Joseph E. Grandville

A revocable living trust can be unfunded, partially funded, or totally funded during the lifetime of its maker; it can also be funded on its maker's death. When estate planning professionals refer to funding, they are referring to property that has actually been placed in a living trust or, more accurately, in the name of the trustees of the trust.

The advantages that result from funding a revocable living trust during the lifetime of the maker are profound:

- Property that is in a revocable living trust does not go through the probate process on the death of the trustmaker.

- Property that is in a revocable living trust can be used to care for the trustmaker and loved ones in the event of the trustmaker's incapacity, without the intervention and control of a court.

- To understand the funded revocable living trust, it is important to contrast it with its unfunded counterpart.

The Unfunded Revocable Living Trust

A living trust that has no assets in it is called an unfunded revocable living trust. Sometimes an unfunded revocable living trust is referred to as an unfunded life insurance trust. It gets this nickname because there is no property placed in the trust when it is created except the *right* of the trust to receive the death proceeds of life insurance on the life of the trustmaker. The trust is funded with only the expectancy of receiving those insurance proceeds. The expectancy of receiving insurance proceeds legally funds the revocable living trust in many states even though, in reality, nothing is in the trust at all.

In those states that require something more than a mere expectancy to establish the trust, professionals generally instruct their clients to place a nominal amount of cash in the trust, such as $10.

Either technique or both techniques used together still result in an unfunded living trust. Why are either of these techniques required? Because in Michigan a trust must have some type of property in it to be valid. Both of these techniques can do the job.

Advocates of the unfunded revocable living trust make the following points in defense of its use:

The trust can receive all life insurance proceeds as well as all other third-party beneficiary contract property. These include pension and profit sharing proceeds paid on the death of the maker.

The revocable living trust can be funded at a later time if the trustmaker gives a durable special power of attorney to others. Durable special powers of attorney are discussed later in this chapter.

Because relatively few deaths result from accidental causes, most trustmakers can generally predict or have notice of their impending demise, and as a result, trustmakers can fund their trusts at that time.

In addition, a pour-over will can transfer property into the trust after the death of the trustmaker.

There can be no doubt that an unfunded revocable living trust is far better than its will counterpart; however, when it is contrasted with its funded counterpart, it leaves much to be desired. There are several problems usually associated with unfunded living trusts.

If the trustmaker dies accidentally or unexpectedly, his or her property will have to go through the probate process before it can ultimately end up in the trust. Thus, a pour-over will guarantees probate on the assets it passes to the unfunded trust. Because most people set up a revocable living trust to avoid probate, not funding the trust pretty much defeats one of its primary purposes.

In our experience, if a trust is not funded from the outset, it does not get funded properly later. If funding is accomplished from the outset, the maker is much more likely to continue funding the trust as new assets are acquired. This new habit assures that at least a great many of a maker's assets will be in the trust upon the maker's disability or death.

A problem that we see much more of is the selling of revocable living trusts at a low cost by living trust companies rather than skilled attorneys. Not only are the trusts themselves woefully inadequate, but they are not funded. Thus a maker ends up with an inferior document that does not avoid probate. However, these trusts are sold as if they were fully funded. The maker and his or her family are misled and probate is not avoided. Consumers should avoid these types of fraudulent schemes.

Funded Revocable Living Trusts

A funded revocable living trust, as its name implies, is a revocable living trust that has within it property owned by the maker. You may be wondering, "How can the trust have the property when the trustmaker still owns it?" The answer is that the property is titled in the trust's name, but the maker still owns the right to use, possess, and enjoy the property. The maker owns the trust and is the beneficiary of the trust and, therefore, really owns the property.

Another way to explain this legal phenomenon is to say that the trustmaker owns equitable title and the trust owns bare legal title. Equitable title is greater than legal title. Regardless of the explanation used, a revocable living trust that is properly funded leaves the ownership and control of the trust property in the hands of the maker.

Funded revocable living trusts have these advantages:

- All property in the trust totally avoids the probate process on the death of its maker.

- The trust assets are instantly available to the maker's beneficiaries pursuant to written instructions.

- Should the maker become incapacitated or be adjudicated mentally incompetent, the trust property can be used to care for the trustmaker and loved ones without the delays, expenses, and publicity associated with court proceedings.

- Funded revocable living trusts take the guesswork out of probate avoidance and avoid the Groucho Marx problem.[1] By funding a revocable living trust, the maker can be assured that trust assets are put to their highest and best use.

- Done properly, the trustmaker should retitle all the trustmaker's property in the name of the trust: for example, "Karen Smith as Trustee of the Karen Smith Trust."

Titling Property Directly in the Trust

In order to place property directly in the name of a trust, the property must be retitled in the name of the trustees of that trust, such as "Karen Smith as Trustee of the Karen Smith Trust." This form of trust funding certainly appears simple and, to most people, is very understandable. It does, however, create some problems.

If real estate is transferred directly into the name of the trust, a Certificate of Trust may have to be recorded. This recording requirement can abrogate the privacy feature of the trust. Because of the growing acceptance of trusts, these filing requirements are becoming much less stringent.

Publicly traded stocks and bonds that are titled directly in the name of a trust sometimes present logistical problems. When the stock

---

1 *Right after a six-week court fight between Groucho's then wife and his own children, who all wanted to be appointed as his "guardian," the Judge ruled in favor of his wife. However, he died a few weeks later and the whole process started over again as a death probate. Many thousands of dollars were needlessly spent and the family was destroyed because Groucho did not have a plan in place.*

or bond is sold, the transfer agent may require that it be provided with a complete and certified copy of the trust. The privacy feature of the trust can then be lost. Just as in real estate, there is much less likelihood of this happening today than even a few short years ago. Generally, only certain provisions of the trust will have to be disclosed, none of which deal with how the trust assets are ultimately to be disposed of.

Safe-deposit boxes taken directly in the name of the trust have the same problem; a complete, certified copy of the trust may have to be kept on file in the institution where the box is located. This obstacle usually can be overcome by giving successor trustees signature authority on the box.

Titling property directly in the name of a trust can present some problems when the trustmaker attempts to dispose of trust property. It is easy to put property directly in the name of a trust, but may be somewhat more difficult to get that property out of the trust. Some of the people with whom the trustees deal with regard to the trust property will want to assure themselves that the trustees do indeed have the right to dispose of the property.

People who deal with trustees may get sweaty palms because without a complete review of the trust document, they can never be sure that the trustee has the power to properly pass title to the trust property. Most trusts are written in legal jargon, and that means that the wary buyer or transfer agent may want to seek the services of an attorney prior to completing any transaction involving trust property.

One technique that is used to reduce or eliminate problems associated with titling property directly in the trust is called Certificate of Trust. This is a short document signed by the trustees and signed by the attorney who prepares the trust, stating that the trust is in existence and that the trustees have the power to transact business on behalf of the trust. Certain provisions of the trust document may be attached to the Certificate, including who the trustees are, their powers, and the signature pages of the trust itself.

Over the years, revocable living trusts have been criticized because of the expense and time it takes to fund them. While this may have been partially true at one time, it is certainly not true now. For the most part, revocable living trusts have been accepted as the estate planning vehicle of choice by a majority of attorneys and other estate planning experts. Banks, stock brokerages, and other financial institutions are set up to expedite transfers into living trusts. Rarely will an individual run into a reputable business or financial institution that will not be willing and able to help fund a living trust. In fact, many financial institutions encourage the funding of revocable living trusts by advertising their expertise in helping to fund the trusts.

Even with the acceptance of living trusts, sometimes it may be more difficult to do business with assets that are titled in the trust name than if they were titled in the name of individual owners or a business. This fact of life should not deter most people from titling property directly in the names of their trusts. More and more, dealing with trusts and trustees is becoming common in the business world. If problems are encountered, there are usually alternate methods of funding that are effective and less likely to cause problems.

Other Methods of Funding a Trust

In Michigan, estate planning professionals have additional techniques available to them to fund a revocable living trust. The four techniques are: durable special powers of attorney, unrecorded deeds, after-death assignments, and POD designations.

Durable Special Powers of Attorney

A trustmaker can give others the power to place the maker's assets into the maker's living trust. This power is given by using a durable special power of attorney. Unlike most powers of attorney, a durable special power of attorney continues even if the maker is incapacitated because of illness or injury. The durable power of attorney is "special" because it limits the power to this single function, funding the trust.

Unrecorded Deeds

In using this technique, the trustmaker deeds real estate to the trustee or successor trustee of the trust, but the deed is not recorded until after the death of the trustmaker. If the trustmaker disposes of the deeded property during lifetime, the unrecorded deed is reclaimed and destroyed. If the trustee at death is a bank or nominee, the existence of the trust does not have to be revealed for title to the deeded property to pass to the trust. Michigan has title standards specifically creating presumptions in favor of the validity of such transfers. The disadvantage of this form of funding is that it may be argued that no effective transfer took place when the deed was signed; however, if the trustmaker's heirs and unsecured creditors are adequately provided for, it is unlikely that anyone would raise an objection. It has been our experience and practice, however, to actually record the deed during the trustmaker's lifetime.

After Death (Postmortem) Assignments

The Michigan Estates and Protected Individuals Code and the Michigan Trust Code provide that many property interests, with the exception of real estate, can be assigned by an owner to a revocable living trust with the transfer not to take effect until after the owner's death. This technique allows a property owner to retain the use and control of property during lifetime and pass that property automatically to a revocable living trust on death. These assignments are not made public.

Postmortem assignments are also effective in transferring closely held (private company) stock certificates and partnership interests into a property owner's revocable living trust. From a practical standpoint, however, this technique does not work very well with publicly traded stocks and bonds.

POD Designations

Generally, Michigan law allows the use of payable-on-death (POD) designations with respect to savings accounts, checking accounts, and certificates of deposit. In creating such an account, the owner simply designates a revocable living trust as the entity that will receive the account proceeds on death. When the owner dies, the account proceeds pass automatically to the trust without the intervention of the probate court.

Conclusion

Funding a revocable living trust is an important aspect of the FWPP. As you can see, there are many techniques available to fund your trust. Please understand that assets that are not in your trust at your death will be subject to the probate process. Assets that are not in the trust if you become incapacitated can be titled in the name of your trust by a durable power of attorney. However, there is no assurance that this method of funding will be effective. Funding your trust when it is set up and as you acquire new property assures you that your trust will work as intended.

PART II

ALIVE AND NOT WELL

6

DISABILITY

Living longer creates good news/bad news and new planning challenges

For all your days prepare,
And meet them ever alike;
When you are the anvil, bear;
When you are the hammer, strike.

Edwin Markham

Estate planning without effective disability planning is no planning at all. Most of us have a much greater chance of becoming disabled in any one year than we do of dying. Yet disability planning is, in our experience, not given the thought and attention it deserves.

There are many types of disabilities, but not all of them require special planning. Loss of a limb, a severe illness, or even a severe injury do not usually prevent a person from being able to take care of himself or herself. However, senility, Alzheimer's disease, psychological problems, drug dependence, automobile or personal accidents, or other factors may make it impossible for an individual to function at a personal or financial level.

The law has long had a method for dealing with those persons who cannot take care of themselves or their financial affairs. Courts, generally the same courts that have jurisdiction over death probate, can declare a person legally incompetent in a proceeding that we call a "living probate." In a living probate, the court appoints two types of agents to care for the incompetent person. The first type is called a personal guardian. A personal guardian acts as the "parent" of the incompetent person. As a surrogate parent, the guardian is charged with taking care of the day-to-day personal needs of the incompetent person. This includes making sure that they are properly fed and housed, that their health needs are met, and that they are supervised, much like a child.

The second type of agent that the court appoints is a financial guardian, sometimes called a conservator. A conservator, who may be a bank, a trust company, or an individual, is in charge of an incompetent person's financial affairs. The financial guardian handles all financial transactions normally handled by the individual. In fact, it is the financial guardian who gives the personal guardian the funds needed to care for the incompetent person. In some cases, the personal guardian and the financial guardian can be the same person; ultimately, it is up to the judge to decide who fulfills these positions. The problem this creates is lack of control which has then shifted to a probate court judge whom you know nothing about and who knows nothing about you.

The personal and financial guardians are appointed and supervised by the court. The personal guardian must give the court periodic reports on the person's physical and mental condition, and the financial guardian must give the court periodic reports about the condition of the person's financial affairs.

The costs of a living probate can be quite high. Attorney fees, court costs, and the costs of retaining a personal and financial guardian are all paid out the incompetent person's assets. Of course, if for some reason the competency of an individual is in dispute, which happens more than most people realize, these costs can skyrocket. In addition, even without controversy, the costs incurred do not go away; the guardians are paid for as long as a person is incompetent, and attorneys must be paid each time a transaction requires work with the court. Even in cases where a spouse or domestic partner or relative is appointed as a guardian, and there are no fees charged by them, significant legal and court fees can be generated.

It has long been recognized that this court-supervised system for disabled persons is cumbersome, expensive, subject to abuse, and, above all, humiliating for the disabled person. The process is public, as are most court proceedings. Because an incompetency hearing can be brought by most anyone who has any connection with an allegedly disabled person, unhappy relatives or even creditors can begin an incompetency hearing. While the majority of these hearings are not controversial, others can be quite messy, lurid affairs.

In the past, there has been abuse reported in the incompetency system. There have been judges who appointed friends to act as financial guardians, excessive fee taking, and, unfortunately, physical and mental abuse of the disabled persons.

Obviously, it makes a great deal of sense to take all action necessary to avoid an incompetency hearing. While there is no effective method for absolutely preventing someone from bringing such a hearing, there are ways to minimize the incentive for doing so. It is one of the functions of estate planning to reduce the likelihood of court involvement when a person is incompetent. In Michigan we have made progress in making it much easier to plan for disabled persons in ways that reduce the chance of court intervention or supervision.

There are four documents that help avoid court intervention when someone becomes disabled. They are:

- Durable power of attorney
- Revocable living trust
- Health care power of attorney
- Living will

Durable Powers of Attorney

Michigan has passed legislation allowing the use of durable powers of attorney. These devices are extremely important in the scheme of estate planning, but are often misunderstood by clients.

Durable powers of attorney are special documents that allow a person who is alive and well today to appoint an agent, called an attorney-in-fact, to handle his or her financial affairs. A durable power of attorney is typically a general power of attorney that does not end if the person granting the power of attorney becomes disabled.

To understand the impact of this planning concept, a little history is necessary. Powers of attorney have long been part of the law in the United States. In a general power of attorney, a person, called a principal, grants to another person or institution (a bank or trust company, for example) the power to act in his or her place. As such, a general power of attorney states, in essence, that the attorney-in-fact can do everything the principal can do. Thus the attorney-in-fact can sign checks, borrow money, make investments, and generally have complete and absolute authority over the principal's finances without his or her consent. A general power of attorney is the ultimate granting of power to another.

General powers of attorney are subject to abuse. In the past, the attorney-in-fact was not held to a particularly high standard of conduct. The result was that some persons holding general powers of attorney were able to squander assets that they were entrusted with, but not be held liable for their errors. A person who grants another person a general power of attorney is placing a great deal of trust in that person and is relying on him or her to be honest, trustworthy, and careful. But reliance is not enough. Michigan imposes higher standards on attorneys-in-fact to reduce abuse, making it easier to sue the person who lost—or took—all the money from a trusting principal. Obviously, this is not a very effective remedy if that person squandered all the funds.

A general power of attorney terminates when a person is adjudicated as mentally incompetent. Of course, this is the time when a power of attorney is most needed.

To make planning easier, Michigan has a statute that allows a power of attorney to continue even if the principal is disabled; these are called *durable powers of attorney*. Granting a durable power of attorney eliminates, at least in theory, the need to have a person adjudicated by a court as mentally incompetent, because the power of attorney survives the incompetency of the principal.

There are some drawbacks in using durable powers of attorney. First, of course, is that the general power is so broad that care must be taken in choosing whom to name as the attorney-in-fact. Remember that durable powers of attorney are in effect when signed, not upon disability. The minute you sign one, the attorney-in-fact can exercise broad powers.

Some attorneys draft "springing" durable powers of attorney. This means that when the principal becomes disabled, as defined in the power of attorney, then it becomes effective.

Another drawback to durable powers of attorney is that they are not universally accepted. Banks, brokerage firms, and other institutions are sometimes wary about accepting durable powers of attorney. They are concerned that the power of attorney may not be in effect because the principal revoked it or that it will be disputed. They often ask for further documentation, or refuse the power of attorney altogether. Michigan requires, by law, the acceptance of durable powers of attorney, but it is not uncommon for large institutions to ignore the law. They do not believe that an attorney-in-fact would initiate a lawsuit over the refusal to honor the power, and these large institutions often feel that refusal causes them less liability than complying might. Slowly, durable powers of attorney are becoming more acceptable, but they still have a way to go.

Finally, a durable power of attorney almost never contains any instructions as to how the attorney-in-fact is supposed to use the principal's funds. If the attorney-in-fact has no guidance, then he or she must use a lot of discretion. Does the attorney-in-fact have the power to make gifts to family members or charity? Can the attorney-in-fact take a fee for services rendered? These are only a few of the issues that may arise. The holder of the power either has to decide, based on his or her best judgment, how to act or, to avoid liability, must refuse to act at all. And, if a power is not specifically set forth in the power of attorney, the holder may not be able to act in any event, in spite of the principal's intent.

We have seen some durable powers of attorney with instructions included in them. They are long, sometimes complex documents. While adding instructions may be a good idea, it is not practical. It is hard enough to get someone to accept a durable power of attorney. It is exponentially more difficult when the power of attorney is long and difficult to read. Most persons then refer the document to their lawyer, and it could be weeks or months before any action is taken to allow or disallow the power of attorney.

We recommend that a *special durable power of attorney* be used in conjunction with a fully funded revocable living trust. A special durable power of attorney restricts the attorney in fact to funding the principal's living trust. It is not a general power of attorney. It is limited in scope and thus far more effective and safe that a general power of attorney. A good living trust will contain effective instructions as to how the trustee is to act on behalf of the trustmaker. Also, the laws governing living trusts and their universal acceptance make using them far easier than relying solely on a power of attorney.

Fully Funded Revocable Living Trusts

Using a special durable power of attorney in concert with a living trust has a number of advantages. A living trust has instructions about how its assets are to be used for the benefit of the trust's maker and his or her family. Trust law is very clear in most respects as to what the trustee can and cannot do. Under a well-drafted trust, the trustee can handle funds in the manner the maker wishes with far less administrative hassle. Almost all financial institutions will accept a trustee's authority with little more than proof of the trust's valid existence and proof that the trustee has the power to act. A certificate of trust signed by the trustee and some excerpts from the trust are sufficient for its acceptance in most cases.

Courts do not, as a rule, have jurisdiction over the assets in a revocable living trust. Thus even if the maker is judged to be incompetent, the court cannot control the assets held in the living trust. Because of this feature, there is less incentive for relatives or "friends" to ask a court to declare someone incompetent; there is no money or power in it if that someone's assets are held in trust, free from court intervention under an incompetency hearing.

In our experience, using a fully funded living trust is far more effective than using a durable power of attorney and a will for disability planning.

A durable power of attorney is not necessary if the living trust is fully funded. However, a special durable power of attorney should be an element of every estate plan as a fail-safe device, in case the maker has not fully funded his or her trust. This is a virtually risk-free approach to planning. If the trust is funded, the durable power is not needed. If the trust is not fully funded, the attorney-in-fact, usually a trustee of the trust in addition to being named in the durable special power of attorney, can transfer assets into the trust and then operate under the trust's instructions.

Health Care Powers of Attorney

A durable power of attorney addresses the financial situation of a disabled person. It does not address the personal side, which may include health care decisions, decisions as to long-term care, and other caregiving decisions. Health care powers of attorney allow you to address these very sensitive issues.

For example, if you are comatose or otherwise unable to make an informed decision as to a certain medical procedure or treatment, your attorney-in-fact under your health care power of attorney is authorized to make that decision. Or, if you need to be institutionalized in a hospital or nursing home and you are not competent to make decisions as to your care, your attorney-in-fact will make that decision consistent with your instructions in a health care power of attorney.

It is possible to add instructions to your health care power of attorney. If you prefer a particular nursing home, if you want to be taken care of at home for as long as possible, or if you prefer one hospital over another, these requests can, depending on your state's laws, be added to your health care power.

You should fully explore with your attorney and other advisors the extent to which you want instructions included in your health care power of attorney so that you feel comfortable with the person or persons you choose to make the decisions and with the guidelines that you include in the power.

Living Wills

Living wills are separate documents that address the situation in which you are terminally ill, in an irreversible coma, or in a permanent vegetative state and there is no likelihood you will recover. The living will is only in effect if you physically or mentally cannot make your desires as to your treatment known.

Generally, a living will states that the maker does not want any procedures that will artificially prolong life, including intravenous feeding, hydration, or medication other than pain relievers. Sometimes, however, a living will states the opposite: that the maker wants his or her physician to take all measures to prolong life.

No matter what your feelings are in this area, a living will is a planning necessity. Not only are your wishes then known by your family, friends, and doctor, but the document also takes the pressure off the ones you love. It is a traumatic experience for a spouse or domestic partner, children, or even friends to be faced with making a decision as to what should be done if you are terminally ill or in a permanent vegetative state. Drafting a living will is a gesture of love that helps alleviate some of the emotional trauma when someone is dying.

Insurance

Everyone should look into the possibility of purchasing health insurance, disability income insurance, and life insurance. Each of these may have a place in your planning. With the constantly rising costs of health care, it is often prudent to purchase insurance to help pay the costs and preserve more of your estate for other purposes.

Health insurance, of course, is extremely important and can be purchased through an employer or directly from a carrier through one of its agents. Disability income insurance, which is often overlooked, is especially important when there is a sole breadwinner in a family. It can be devastating to a family when the primary income earner is sick or injured and cannot provide income.

Finally, life insurance may be a very important part of estate planning. There are numerous policy types and companies offering those policies. You should always include a top-notch insurance professional in your planning team so that you can make an informed and wise decision as to whether you need life insurance and what kind best fits your needs.

With the ability of modern science to allow people to live longer, disability planning is even more important. One of the fastest-growing age groups in the United States is those who are over 100 years of age! As we live longer, we are not necessarily living better. We need more care, not less. That is one of the main reasons why disability planning in all aspects is so vitally important to the overall estate planning process, and why each member of the estate planning team must be intimately involved in such planning.

It is imperative that an estate plan, no matter how modest, address disability. Without disability planning, you are left purely to a legal system that, try as it might, cannot replace instructions left by you to be implemented by the people or institutions of your choosing.

To summarize, at a minimum, your basic estate plan should include:
- A special durable power of attorney,
- A fully funded revocable living trust,
- A power of attorney for health care, and
- A living will.

7

LIVING PROBATE

Loss of Control
Can be Avoided.

We have met the enemy...and they is us.

Pogo, Walt Kelly

Overview—The Growing Importance of Planning for Incapacity

Longevity in the United States is increasing; as a result, the possibility that an individual will experience a period of incapacity during his or her lifetime is much greater now than it was just a few years ago. The leading causes of death among the elderly—heart disease, cancer, and strokes—are likely to involve a period of incapacity and to require long-term care[2].

---

2 *National Center for Health Statistics, Health, United States, 2008 with Chartbook 219 (2009).*

In 2004, approximately 1.3 million persons sixty-five years of age and over, representing 3.6 percent of the older population, were in nursing homes.[3] Women are more likely than men to become nursing home residents, and the likelihood of becoming a nursing home resident increases for both sexes with age. In 2004, 138 out of 1,000 persons eighty-five years of age and over were nursing home residents.[4] In light of these facts, a good estate plan that recognizes the need and provides for asset management in the event of a disability is in the interests of both the grantor and his or her family.

Planning for disability is particularly important because of the increasingly complex investment alternatives. Both the number of investment alternatives and the factors to be considered when managing finances have become more complicated, making the planning for management of assets in the event of incapacity critical.

Advantages of Planning with a Living Trust

Asset Management during Incapacity

Although other alternatives such as jointly titled bank accounts, joint investment accounts, and powers of attorney can provide another individual access to assets, they cannot provide the same level of management and distribution direction as a well-drafted living trust agreement. The trustmaker may prefer that an individual trustee or a professional (corporate) trustee—or both—serve as the acting trustee (or cotrustees) in the event of incapacity. The trustmaker may also prefer to divide management and investment decisions between individual and professional trustees. For example, an individual successor trustee may be appropriate to manage a business or farm held by the trust, but a corporate trustee may be more appropriate to make tax elections and manage the liquid trust assets. Also, with the passage of the Michigan Trust Code (MTC), the trustmaker can name a trust protector with defined duties and powers to add flexibility to the trustee arrangement. Through the use of a living trust, the trustmaker, while able to do so, can establish a plan that provides for a significant degree of control over investment activities and decisions occurring during the time after he or she has become incapacitated.

3 Id. at 155, 392

4 Id. at 392

Avoidance of Court Intervention

A well-drafted, funded living trust can avoid the need for court intervention in the event of incapacity. If a living trust is in existence but has not been funded at the time of incapacity, it can only be funded thereafter by use of a well-drafted, durable power of attorney.

Ways to Provide for Incapacity

1. **Define *Incapacity* in the Trust Document and the Succession of Trustees**

   A living trust can provide that the successor trustee will take control in the event of the trustmaker's incapacity. If a trust document uses the term *incapacity* to describe the triggering point for the succession of trustees or for the loss of other power by the trustmaker, the term should be defined in the document or a court may have to become involved to make the decision. Moreover, the trustmaker will probably feel more comfortable having the term defined in the document.

2. **The Estates and Protected Individuals Code (EPIC)**

   EPIC, now included in the Michigan Trust Code (MTC), defines an incapacitated individual as "an individual who is impaired by reason of mental illness, mental deficiency, physical illness or disability, chronic use of drugs, chronic intoxication, or other cause, not including minority, to the extent of lacking sufficient understanding or capacity to make or communicate informed decisions." This is the standard the probate court will apply to determine whether a guardian should be appointed to make personal decisions for the individual. It is also the standard that a court would use when determining incapacity if a living trust agreement used the term *incapacity* but did not provide a definition of it or a specific procedure for determining it.

3. **Distinguish Incapacity from Incompetency**

   Most trust documents that provide for a transition in the event of incapacity are intended to apply when an individual becomes unable to effectively manage his or her assets because of decreased mental capacity, disability, or physical illness. The term *incompetency* should not be substituted for the term *incapacity* for this purpose in the trust document because most definitions of *incompetency* require a more significant loss of mental abilities. Although there are many definitions of *legal incompetency,* the most common ones are those used to determine whether an individual can stand trial and whether an individual must be institutionalized to prevent danger to himself or others. Many trustmakers who would be determined incapacitated or unable to effectively manage their affairs or act in the best interests of a trust would not be found legally incompetent.

4. **Determination by Individual, Trust Protector, or Panel**
    An additional alternative is to provide that another named individual, a trust protector, or a panel, by unanimous (or majority) vote determines when it is no longer in the best interests of the trust for the trustmaker to be trustee. The trustmaker may desire a more specific standard of incapacity to be set forth in the trust document if this alternative is to be used.

    If the panel approach is used, the trustmaker may want to specify how many members are to be on the panel and who those members are. Panel members could include family members, medical professionals, income beneficiaries, professional advisors, successor trustees, or any combination of these. The trust should state whether the determination requires a unanimous or majority vote. Further, the trust agreement could specify whether voting should be by secret ballot or show of hands, and, if by secret ballot, who will count the ballots.

The panel approach may meet with some resistance by third parties who are reluctant or unwilling to recognize the new trustee unless these provisions grant the panel discretion to determine incapacity. A trustmaker may attempt to revoke the trust if he or she disagrees with the committee's determination and has not been found to be legally incompetent.

Effect of Incapacity on
Trust Management

Duties of Successor Trustee

Most living trusts provide that a successor trustee has all of the powers and authority of an initial trustee without any court intervention. After qualification, it provides that every trustee has the broad powers and authority granted by law and the trust document. The trust should provide that during a period in which the trustmaker is incapable of caring for himself or herself, the trustee will distribute assets to the trustmaker, the trustmaker's spouse or domestic partner, or other dependents.

Grantor's Right to Amend Trust

Under the MTC, the trustmaker may generally revoke or amend a trust unless the terms of the trust expressly provide that the trust is irrevocable. Even though a trustmaker may be legally incapacitated and unable to manage assets, unless it is specifically provided for in the trust, he or she does not automatically lose the right to amend or revoke the trust and thereby change the disposition of assets. Rather, it is presumed that a trustmaker intends to retain the right to revoke or amend the trust as long as he or she has the capacity to make a disposition. The MTC, effective April 1, 2010, has changed the standard for legal capacity to make a will from "a person of sound mind" to an individual who:

1. Has the ability to understand that he or she is providing for the disposition of his or her property after death.

2. Has the ability to know the nature and extent of his or her property.

3. Knows the natural objects of his or her bounty, i.e. children and grandchildren.

4. Has the ability to understand in a reasonable manner the general nature and effect of his or her act in signing the will. Under the MTC, the capacity required to create, amend, or revoke a trust is the same as that required to make a will.

Coordination with Durable Power of Attorney

A living trust is a more effective tool for planning than is a durable power of attorney. This is true for several reasons. A major reason is that assets titled in the name of a trust will avoid probate, whereas the authority under a durable power of attorney ends at death. Moreover, the formality of titling assets into a trust may help in the management of and accounting for those assets. A trust can contain more thorough administrative provisions and specific dispositive provisions after death than a durable power of attorney.

However, there are several important reasons for using a general durable power of attorney in conjunction with a living trust. Accordingly, even if a comprehensive living trust is included in the estate plan, a carefully tailored general durable power of attorney will greatly enhance it.

Uses of Durable Powers of Attorney in Conjunction with Grantor Trusts

Funding a Trust

A provision for funding a trust can be the most useful provision in a limited funding durable power of attorney for a trustmaker of a living trust. By allowing an agent to transfer assets to the trustee, management can continue without court interference after a trustmaker has been deemed incapacitated. As a practical matter, often a trustmaker may resist immediate trust funding or inadvertently fail to thoroughly fund the trust. If a durable power of attorney allows trust funding, these problems or oversights can be repaired without court intervention.

Creating, Amending, or Revoking a Trust: Other Uses—Gifts

By including a power to gift under the limited and miscellaneous general durable power of attorney, an individual can allow for reduction of federal estate tax through reduction of the potential taxable estate of an incapacitated person or through continuation of a trustmaker's historical gifting program.

Currently, if a power of attorney does not specifically include a power to gift, the holder of the power may be prevented from making an effective gift. Michigan law makes it clear that regarding all durable powers of attorney executed after October 1, 2012, an agent does not have the authority to gift without express language in a power of attorney.

Other Personal Decisions

Most trustees (especially corporate trustees) are not comfortable exercising authority over personal decisions such as medical care, so the power to make medical and other personal decisions is more appropriately given in a durable power of attorney for health care (also known as a designation of patient advocate in Michigan statutes). An individual acting under a durable power of attorney can show authority by revealing the provisions of the power of attorney and does not have to disclose the confidential nature of the dispositive provisions of the trust.

For a durable power of attorney for health care to be valid in Michigan, the power of attorney must comply with a number of statutory provisions. These include the requirement that the designated agent (patient advocate) must sign an acceptance to the designation.

The durable power of attorney for health care includes specific language authorizing the withholding or withdrawal of specific treatments, including feeding tubes, cardiopulmonary resuscitation, and respirators. The durable power of attorney also expresses a preference for medication to alleviate suffering even if it might hasten death.

You should also include a HIPAA form with authorization for all health care providers and others with protected health information to disclose medical records to the patient advocate under the Health Insurance Portability and Accountability Act of 1996 (HIPAA), and any other statute or rule. Because a patient advocate is authorized to act only when the patient is unable to make medical decisions, there may be a time period when the patient advocate needs access to medical records but does not have the right to access them. One solution is to also grant such authority to the agent under the financial power of attorney.

The durable power of attorney for health care may also include the authority to make anatomical gifts.

PART III

ONE OF US DIES

8

PLANNING FOR A SPOUSE OR DOMESTIC PARTNER

An Endless Buffet

It is that extra creation that stands hurt and baffled at the place of death...Being human wanting children and sunlight and breath to go on, forever.

Christopher Leach

Gathering Information

The first step of the FWPP, and the key ingredient to proper planning and drafting, is gathering complete, accurate information about you, your family, and the financial circumstances. Consequently, the initial interview is very important, and the planner should develop a complete checklist of questions. In addition to the usual questions, such as the names, addresses, and ages of you, your spouse or domestic partner, and decedents, as well as you and your spouse or domestic partner's financial information, you should answer the following questions:

- Have you been married before? If so, do you have any children from a former marriage?

- Do your children expect to receive benefits from your former spouse or domestic partner?

- Do you have any children of a subsequent marriage? Will all of your children be treated equally?

- Has your spouse or domestic partner been married before? If so, does your spouse or domestic partner have children of a prior marriage?

- Will you treat your spouse or domestic partner's children as your own? Have you adopted, or will you adopt, the children?

- Is your spouse or domestic partner or are any of your children disabled or in poor health? Is it possible that the person with a disability would qualify for public assistance, and if so, should steps be taken to ensure that an inheritance will not destroy that qualification?

- What are your goals for your children? Have your children completed their education? If not, what are their educational goals? Should a common trust fund be used to educate all of your children before dividing the residue, or should a specific amount be set aside for each child who is under the age of 21 to fund his or her support and education?

- Are your children employed? Do they have adequate income, assets, or both?

- Are any children deceased with spouse or domestic partners surviving? Do you want a deceased child's spouse or domestic partner to share in your estate?

- Do you want your spouse or domestic partner to share in your estate? Is your spouse or domestic partner able and willing to manage assets? Are you and your spouse or domestic partner's views regarding disposition of assets the same? Do you fear the effects of your spouse or domestic partner's remarriage following your death?

- Are you and your spouse or domestic partner U.S. citizens?

(See Appendix A, Preparation for Planning: Getting Organized)

These questions are examples of the issues you should discuss with your attorney.

Establishing Objectives

The next step in the FWPP is to establish your objectives and select the appropriate estate planning techniques. Your objectives may be determined by tax considerations, by the family situation, by personal goals, by financial circumstances, and to some extent by the estate planning technique itself.

For example, taxable estates equal to or less than the applicable exclusion, what we refer to as the IRS grocery store coupon amount, and with no adjusted taxable gifts, pay no federal estate tax. For decedents who die in 2014, the applicable exclusion/IRS grocery store coupon amount is $5,430,000. In estates over the applicable exclusion/IRS grocery store coupon amount, your objectives may include minimizing estate taxes by taking advantage of both the applicable exclusion/IRS grocery store coupon amount and the unlimited marital deduction. Just like your real grocery store, the IRS grocery store has a "double coupon day." The marital deduction/IRS grocery store double coupon day is the federal estate tax deduction for property passing to or for the benefit of the surviving spouse or domestic partner. If the spouse or domestic partner is not a U.S. citizen, no marital deduction/IRS grocery store double coupon day is allowed unless a qualified domestic trust is used.

Taking advantage of these two tax provisions usually involves use of a trust that on the death of the trustmaker is divided into two sub-buckets or "lock boxes." One portion is held in a trust, known as a family trust, and is used to shelter the applicable exclusion/IRS grocery store coupon amount. This portion passes without estate tax consequences, even on the death of the surviving spouse or domestic partner. The balance of the estate passes to or for the benefit of the surviving spouse or domestic partner either outright or in a marital trust. This portion is not taxed until the death of the surviving spouse or domestic partner, when it is taxed as part of the surviving spouse or domestic partner's estate.

You and your spouse or domestic partner may also want to use trusts to provide management assistance for the surviving spouse or domestic partner and children or to permit the propertied spouse or domestic partner to shift assets to the non-propertied spouse or domestic partner while continuing to manage those assets.

From the signing of the trust agreement until the date of the trustmaker's death, the trust will benefit the trustmaker. The trust can hold all types of assets and is designed to distribute income and principal at the trustmaker's direction. If the trustmaker becomes disabled, the trustee will usually have discretion to distribute income and principal to provide for the health, support, maintenance, welfare, and comfort of the trustmaker and his or her dependents.

On the trustmaker's death, the trust becomes irrevocable and the client's estate plan becomes fixed. Thereafter, the trust assumes the client's role of providing for his or her spouse or domestic partner and children and providing for the disposition of his or her estate.

Marital Deduction/IRS Grocery Store Double Coupon Day

Portion of the Estate

You can take advantage of the marital deduction/IRS grocery store double coupon day by an outright transfer directly to the spouse or domestic partner or by a trust for the spouse or domestic partner's benefit that satisfies the marital deduction/IRS grocery store double coupon day requirements. Sometimes, we use this provision for the following planning goals even though your total gross estate does not exceed the coupon amounts.

Whether outright or in a trust, the transfer of property to or for the benefit of a surviving spouse or domestic partner may be accomplished through a variety of mechanisms.

Distribution to a Spouse or Domestic Partner Outright

After the trust assets are allocated and divided into the marital portion and the family portion, the trust can direct that the marital portion be distributed to the surviving spouse or domestic partner outright.

The outright distribution alternative is used when:

1. The client has confidence in his or her spouse or domestic partner's ability to manage assets.

2. The client and spouse or domestic partner have substantially the same goals concerning disposition of assets.

3. The client wants his or her spouse or domestic partner to have complete freedom over the assets.

4. The client's spouse or domestic partner is in good physical and mental health.

5. The client and spouse or domestic partner plan to have the spouse or domestic partner make lifetime gifts to reduce the spouse or domestic partner's estate.

6. There is a likelihood that the amount in the trust will not be adequate to justify the separate record-keeping involved.

7. There are no children of a prior marriage.

If the above situations are not present, you should consider using one of the alternatives that follow. In particular, an outright distribution is normally not used where you want to ensure that children of a prior or current marriage receive the assets of the estate.

Life Estate with General Power of Appointment

The life estate with a general power of appointment trust provides many of the benefits available with the outright distribution alternative. This type of marital trust is used when you:

1. Want to ensure that your spouse or domestic partner will have assistance in managing assets during his or her lifetime.

2. Do not wish to restrict the surviving spouse or domestic partner's power to dispose of trust assets.

3. Wish to provide the spouse or domestic partner with the power to appoint assets of the trust during his or her lifetime to reduce the trust estate.

4. Do not want to provide an outright transfer, hoping that the property will stay in the trust and end up with the beneficiaries the spouse or domestic partner has designated. This trust is not used when the client wishes to control the ultimate disposition of the assets, particularly in situations where there are children of a prior or current marriage.

Qualifying for the Marital Deduction/
IRS "Grocery Store Double Coupon Day"

To qualify for the marital deduction/IRS grocery store double coupon day, the trust must satisfy the following requirements:

1. The surviving spouse or domestic partner must be entitled for life to all of the income from the property or from a specific portion of the property, payable at least annually.

2. The surviving spouse or domestic partner must have the power to appoint (give) the entire interest, or a specific portion of it, in favor of himself or herself, his or her estate, or either.

3. The power to appoint must be exercisable by the surviving spouse or domestic partner.

4. No other person may have any power to appoint (give) any part of the interest to any person other than the surviving spouse or domestic partner.

Income Provision

The trust will contain an income provision, a principal provision, and a general power-of-appointment provision. The income provision will require that all income be paid to the spouse or domestic partner for his or her life. The income provision should also contain a restriction that the trustee will not invest in life insurance policies and a provision that the spouse or domestic partner can direct the trustee to convert unproductive assets to productive assets. The purpose of this last provision is to protect the surviving spouse or domestic partner's right to income. A personal residence and other personal-use property may be held in the marital trust even though it will not produce income.

Invasion of Principal

The trust can, although it is not required to, contain a provision permitting the invasion of principal. The provision regarding principal can require the trustee to distribute principal if the trustee determines that the income and other assets available to the spouse or domestic partner are insufficient to maintain the spouse or domestic partner's standard of living or properly provide for the spouse or domestic partner's health, support, welfare, and comfort. This provision is important in case income is insufficient. The discretion given the trustee may vary or even be eliminated depending on the circumstances, but the trustee may not be permitted to invade principal for anyone other than the surviving spouse or domestic partner.

These provisions often direct the trustee to invade the principal of the marital trust before invading the principal of the family trust for the trustmaker's spouse or domestic partner's benefit unless the marital trust has been exhausted or unless, in the trustee's discretion, invasion of the martial trust is impractical or inadvisable. This type of provision will help preserve the family trust for the beneficiaries and will work to reduce the marital trust, which is subject to estate tax on the spouse or domestic partner's death.

What is a "QTIP" and Why Would I Need One
If I Don't Have Wax In My Ears?

A Qualified Terminable Interest Property (QTIP) trust is a marital trust that has a life estate in it for the surviving spouse or domestic partner. They are used less and less today because of the flexibility inherent in the QTIP trust. For example, if you are willing to give your spouse or domestic partner a general power of appointment, it might be easier to simply make an outright gift. One reason for not doing this might be a fear that the survivor will be disabled at the time of the first death, in which event the trust would provide protection.

The QTIP Trust
How Much Control is on Each End?

The QTIP trust is used when you:

1. Desire to restrict the distribution of assets, such as in situations where there are children from a prior or current marriage.

2. Fear that the surviving spouse or domestic partner could be taken advantage of or influenced by others.

3. You may want to defer the decision to claim the maximum marital deduction/IRS grocery store double coupon day.

A QTIP trust must satisfy the following requirements of the Internal Revenue Code:

1. The surviving spouse or domestic partner must be entitled to all of the income from the property (or a specified portion of it) for life, payable at least annually.

2. No person may be empowered to appoint any part of the property to someone other than the surviving spouse or domestic partner, unless the power is exercisable at or after the surviving spouse or domestic partner's death.

3. An election must be made to treat the property as qualified terminable interest property.

The QTIP trust will normally contain a tax election provision, an income provision, a principal provision, a payment-of-taxes provision, and a provision for the disposition of the property following the spouse or domestic partner's death.

Income Provision

The income provision requires that all income be paid to the spouse or domestic partner for his or her lifetime. The income must be paid at least annually but may be paid more frequently.

Invasion of Principal

The QTIP trust can, although it is not required to, contain a provision permitting the invasion of principal. The provision regarding principal will allow the trustee to distribute principal if the trustee determines that income and other assets are insufficient to maintain the spouse or domestic partner's standard of living or to properly provide for his or her health, support, welfare, and comfort.

Five and Five Power

If a "five and five" power is included in the trust, the spouse or domestic partner is given the right to annually withdraw from principal the greater of $5,000 or five percent of the trust on the last day of the year in which the withdrawal is requested. This power is very useful because it not only provides the spouse or domestic partner with some feeling of control over the trust assets but it also allows the spouse or domestic partner to reduce his or her estate by making some lifetime gifts.

Distribution on Death of Spouse or Domestic Partner

The trust can contain a distribution provision directing that the trust funds be distributed to specific beneficiaries of the trustmaker's trust. For example, the trustmaker's children, grandchildren, stepchildren, or others.

Questions for You to Consider

With an understanding of the marital deduction/IRS grocery store double coupon day and the reasons for using various techniques, you should be prepared to answer the following questions:

1. Do you want to take full advantage of your coupon? To the extent your estate is otherwise taxable, do you want to take full advantage of the marital deduction/double coupon?

2. Do you want to leave the marital deduction/IRS grocery store double coupon day share to your spouse or domestic partner outright or in trust?

3. Do you want to use the QTIP trust, or a combination of both kinds of trusts?

4. If you want to use a QTIP trust, who will receive the property on your spouse or domestic partner's death?

5. Do you want to provide for a special power of appointment or do you want to specify who the beneficiaries will be?

Family Portion of the Estate

The family trust can be established for the benefit of the spouse or domestic partner, the spouse or domestic partner and descendants, the descendants, or any other recipient. Family trusts are generally used when you want:

1. To save the family federal estate taxes.

2. To make sure that your family members are provided for.

3. Have the property pass to your descendants.

The family trust can save the family a considerable amount of federal estate taxes. Assets held in a family trust are included in your gross estate, IRC 2038, and are subject to estate tax. However, the estate tax is usually offset by your coupon, which means that assets equal to or less than the coupon pass free of federal estate tax.

Trust for Spouse or Domestic Partner and Descendants

If you want the surviving spouse or domestic partner to receive the benefits of the family trust, there are three basic alternatives:

1. The spouse or domestic partner will receive all of the net income.

2. The trustee may be given discretion to sprinkle income among the spouse or domestic partner and descendants.

3. Income will be accumulated and added to principal.

Trust for Spouse or Domestic Partner: Payment of All Income

To provide for the payment of all the net income of the non-marital trust, the trust would simply provide: "Trustee shall pay net income to or for the benefit of my spouse or domestic partner." The income received from the trust is included in the spouse or domestic partner's gross income and reported on his or her income tax return. In deciding whether to use this alternative, the estate planner must consider the ages of the spouse or domestic partner and children and the size of the estate.

Sprinkle Income Provision

In lieu of paying all of the income to the spouse or domestic partner, the trust can provide a sprinkling-of-income provision. This provision provides the trustee with discretion to distribute the income among those beneficiaries named by the trustmaker. Therefore, the trust could direct the trustee to pay all of the net income to one or more of the trustmaker's descendants as the trustee deems appropriate under the circumstances existing at each date of distribution, taking into account the potential recipient's economic needs, best interests and welfare, income tax brackets, and availability of other resources. The provision should also state that these distributions can be unequal amounts and can exclude members of the class to be benefited.

Another tax advantage of giving the trustee the right to sprinkle income is that the income is taxed to the recipient. The trustee may cause the income to be taxed to a beneficiary who is in a lower tax bracket. This may be a very important advantage. If the spouse or domestic partner subsequently marries a person with high income, the trustee can pay all of the income to the beneficiaries other than the spouse or domestic partner. If the trust provided for the payment of all income to the spouse or domestic partner and the spouse or domestic partner did not need it, the spouse or domestic partner would nevertheless be taxed on it.

There are also nontax advantages to a sprinkling provision. Giving the trustee the right to sprinkle the income allows the trustee to function as a parental substitute, paying income to those beneficiaries who need it and excluding those who do not. The sprinkling feature also operates as a protection against creditors. Creditors cannot reach the beneficiary's interest because the amount that the beneficiary receives depends on the trustee's exercise of his or her discretion.

Accumulation of Income

The family trust can provide for the accumulation of income and the distribution of the accrued income by means of principal distributions. This can be accomplished by simply providing that "the net income of the trust shall be accumulated and thereafter treated as principal." This type of provision is often used when the client's spouse or domestic partner has ample income of his or her own or when the client does not want the spouse or domestic partner to share in the non-marital trust except when the invasion of principal is necessary. The advantage of this type of provision is that it allows the family trust to grow.

Distribution of Principal

The provision regarding the distribution of principal of the family trust usually provides that the trustee may distribute principal to the beneficiaries only under certain circumstances. Therefore, the trustee could be authorized to distribute the principal of the family trust to or for the benefit of the grantor's spouse or domestic partner or descendants if the trustee determines that the income and other property available to any such beneficiary is insufficient to provide for the beneficiary's health, maintenance, or support or is insufficient for the education of the trustmaker's descendants when the spouse or domestic partner is beneficiary and trustee.

Spouse or Domestic Partner's Remarriage

There are several ways that the family trust can be drafted to deal with the spouse or domestic partner's remarriage:

1. Conversion of mandatory payment of income to a discretionary sprinkling provision.

2. Permanent removal of the spouse or domestic partner as beneficiary of the sprinkling provision upon remarriage.

3. Removal of the spouse or domestic partner as beneficiary of a sprinkling provision only during the remarriage.

Conversion of Mandatory Payment of Income to Discretionary Sprinkling Provision

The family trust may provide that the mandatory payout of income converts to a discretionary sprinkle provision during any period that the spouse or domestic partner is remarried. The income provision would then provide that the trustee will pay all of the net income of the trust to the spouse or domestic partner for those periods during which the spouse or domestic partner is not remarried, and while the spouse or domestic partner is remarried, the trustee may pay income to the spouse or domestic partner, the trustmaker's descendants, or both, as the trustee deems appropriate under the circumstances existing at each distribution, taking into account the economic needs, best interests, welfare, income tax brackets, availability of other resources, and the guidelines provided for invasions of principal such as for health, maintenance, support, and education for each recipient.

Removal of Spouse or Domestic Partner from Sprinkling Trust

The family trust could provide the spouse or domestic partner with benefits as long as the spouse or domestic partner remains single. If he or she remarries, the trust could remove the spouse or domestic partner as the beneficiary. The removal provision eliminates the possible pressure by the spouse or domestic partner's new spouse or domestic partner for the spouse or domestic partner, as trustee, to distribute income and principal, and allows the spouse or domestic partner, as a trustee, to continue to care for the children. The trust could provide for a permanent removal or for removal for only the period of remarriage. This latter provision is beneficial in case the spouse or domestic partner is later widowed or divorced, and it also shows the trustmaker's love and concern for the spouse or domestic partner.

Limited Distribution of Principal

The family trust may also provide for discretionary distribution of principal. This type of provision would provide that the trustee may distribute any or all of the principal of the trust to or for the benefit of the spouse or domestic partner or any of the trustmaker's descendants if the trustee determines that the income and other property available to any such beneficiary is insufficient to provide for the beneficiary's health, maintenance, or support or is insufficient for the education of the trustmaker's descendants.

As a guide to the trustee in exercising its discretion, the provision may state the trustmaker's intent that during the remarriage of the spouse or domestic partner, the trustmaker still wishes to provide, after looking to other resources (including the earnings or potential earnings of the new spouse or domestic partner), the support for his or her spouse or domestic partner and family to the extent it is needed to maintain the spouse or domestic partner's accustomed standard of living, but that the trustmaker does not wish to provide support or benefits for the new spouse or domestic partner.

Trusts for Children of a Prior Marriage

The family trust can be established for the benefit of your spouse or domestic partner and children of a previous marriage, or exclusively for the children. If the trust is established for the spouse or domestic partner and children, there may be a need to protect the interests of the children. This protection may be accomplished in a number of ways:

1. Requiring the spouse or domestic partner to use his or her own funds before the trust principal may be used on his or her behalf.

2. Setting limits on the invasions of principal for the benefit of the spouse or domestic partner (such as that only twenty-five percent of principal may be used).

3. Prohibiting invasion of principal altogether. A trust provision of this type is used when the client wants to make sure that the nonmarital assets will end up in the hands of the children but is still concerned about providing for his or her spouse or domestic partner.

Questions for You to Consider

Here are some questions you should be prepared to answer:

1. Whom do you want to receive the income of the family trust: your spouse or domestic partner, your spouse or domestic partner and children, only your children, or other relatives?

2. Do you want the income paid only to your spouse or domestic partner? Do you want the income sprinkled among your spouse or domestic partner and children? Or do you want the income accumulated for your spouse or domestic partner's life and added to principal?

3. If you want the income paid to your spouse or domestic partner, do you want the trust to provide that it will convert from mandatory payout to discretionary payout if your spouse or domestic partner remarries?

4. On your spouse or domestic partner's death, do you want the family trust assets to be distributed according to the directions of your trust? Or do you want to give your spouse or domestic partner a special power of appointment for purposes of post-death planning?

Distribution on Death

After the spouse or domestic partner's death, there are two basic methods to determine when to divide the assets remaining in the family trust into shares for the children based on the idea of protecting the assets from any potential "Creditors and Predators." One method provides for a division of the assets into sub-buckets or lock boxes when the youngest child attains a specified age or accomplishes a specific goal such as graduating from college. The other method involves setting up a lifetime protected lock box share for each beneficiary.

Separate Trust for Each Child

This type of trust provision provides for the immediate division of trust assets into sub-buckets or lock boxes and the establishment of separate trusts for each portion, typically, one for each child of the trustmaker who is living at that time and one for each child of the trustmaker who has died but is survived by grandchildren living at that time. The trust can have a limitless variety of distribution alternatives based on a "Spectrum of Protection™" ranging from zero protection to complete protection when using a professional trustee. For example, the trust can provide for immediate distribution (the Corvette University scholarship fund), distribution at a specified age, or multiple distributions (unwrapping the candy bar at the picnic so the ants can eat it). The trust can also require the trustee to transfer to the beneficiary of the separate trust the part of the principal to which the beneficiary is entitled by reason of having attained a specified age for distribution. Or, the lifetime full access, liberal access, conservative access, or convenience "Creditor and Predator" protection trust.

Each separate trust contains an income provision and a principal distribution provision that governs until the time arrives for outright distribution of principal. The income provision is usually discretionary so that income can be accumulated if not needed. The principal distribution provision usually permits the distribution of principal for health, maintenance, support, education, buying a home, investing in a business, and emergencies. The trust can also be restricted to provide only for the health, education, maintenance, and support of the beneficiary. Each trust also contains a provision for distribution at a specified age or in specified fractions at specified ages or as a lifetime protected trust. Finally, each trust should contain a provision that deals with the premature death of the beneficiary by providing who will receive the property.

Common Trust Fund Until the Youngest Child is a Certain Age, or Graduates from College— The "Chicken Soup Pot Trust"

The common trust allows for the support and education of the children from the entire principal of the trust. It is often used when

1. The older children have already received these benefits and it may be inequitable not to provide similar benefits for the younger children.

2. The children are all minors.

3. You want the entire trust principal to be available to care for the needs of the children because some children's needs may be greater than other children's needs.

Under this type of trust, the assets would be held in a continuing or common trust until the youngest child reaches a specified age or until some event, such as graduation from college, occurs. Any age can be used. Also, the trust could continue until the youngest child attains a certain age or graduates from college, whichever occurs first. Adding the age factor to the event of graduating from college helps to keep a "professional student" from depleting his or her siblings' inheritance.

The continuing trust would ordinarily give the trustee discretion to distribute funds for education, support, and health. The trustee should be instructed to care for each child based on his or her needs as measured against the income or other assets available. Some children may need more income than other children. The provisions should also instruct the trustee to assist the guardian of the children in caring for them and in protecting the guardian from suffering significant financial burden by reason of the appointment. This is important because the guardian will now have additional children to feed, clothe, shelter, and drive to various events. The guardian may even have to build an addition onto the home or buy a larger vehicle.

Finally, the trust should provide that when the named event occurs, the continuing trust would be divided into and administered as separate trusts.

Lifetime Trust for Children: "The Lock Box Trust"

Under this type of trust, the trustee has the discretion to pay some or all of the net income to the children during their lifetimes and has discretion to invade principal for the children's benefit. On the death of each child, the child's share passes to the child's issue, to named individuals, or across to the other beneficiaries.

The trust usually contains a provision that divides the trust assets into sub-buckets or lock boxes, one for each child who is then living and one for each child who has died but has issue when living. The sub-buckets or lock boxes set aside for the living children are then held in trust for their lifetimes. The trust has an income provision and a standard for distribution-of-principal provision. These provisions allow a variety of methods of income and principal distributions and can be designed to benefit the children or the children and their descendants.

The standard for distribution-of-principal provision could provide the trustee with discretion to pay the beneficiary (or his or her descendants) or expend for their benefit such part of the principal as the trustee deems desirable, taking into consideration the potential beneficiary's needs, best interests, and welfare, including the desirability of augmenting the beneficiary's estate, his or her ability to manage assets prudently, and any other factors the trustee considers pertinent. This provision works especially well, when, in the opinion of the trustmaker, the beneficiary is capable of being their own trustee, with a co-trustee of their choice limited to one or more of the following; a licensed attorney; a licensed CPA; or a person over the age thirty.

On the death of the children, the trust can provide for immediate distribution of each child's trust to his or her children. The portion set aside for the issue of a deceased child can be distributed in a lump sum at a specified age or at specified fractions at specified ages, or can be kept in the life time share.

Trust for a Disabled Child

In the context of trusts for disabled children, there are at least two basic alternatives available: support trusts and discretionary supplemental trust designed to supplement government benefits. A Support trust is a trust providing that the trustee will pay or only apply so much of the income and principal as is necessary for the education or support of the beneficiary. A Support trust is usually used when the client is a larger estate and is designed to provide for the child's full support. The discretionary supplemental trust is a trust design to supplement the public assistance provided to the beneficiary. It normally provides that trustee will pay to or apply for a beneficiary only so much of the income and principal as the trustee in his or her discretion sees fit.

Family Reunion Atomic Bomb Disaster Provisions

As part of the planning process you should decide on an alternative disposition of trust assets should everyone predecease you. Although the chance of this ever happening is small, good planning requires it. There are various ways to provide for this alternative disposition. For example, the trust could provide that if there is no one to take the assets under the terms of the trust, the trustee will pay half of the assets to those persons who would have taken the trust maker's estate if he or she had died intestate, or without a will, and the other half to those persons who would've taken the trustmaker's spouse or domestic partner's estate had he or she died without a will, or intestate. This type of provision reflects the attitude that the property is treated as if it were equally owned by each spouse or domestic partner. Or the trust could provide that if there is no one to receive under the trust agreement, the trustee would pay the trust funds to certain individuals, certain charities, or a combination of any of these. If you choose to designate certain individuals you will also need to address who will get the property in the event those individuals are not alive at the time.

Questions for You

1. After your spouse or domestic partner's death, do you want the trust divided into sub-buckets or lock boxes at that time when your youngest child reaches a certain age, and if so, what age?

2. If you want the trust divided when your youngest child reaches a specified age and there are several years between the youngest and the oldest child, do you want the older children to be allowed to have distributions before that division into shares, and if so how much?

3. After the division into separate shares for your children, what type of distribution do you want for them? For example, payment of the principal at a certain age or at specified ages over time, or the right to withdraw certain fractions at specified ages? Or would you prefer that the assets be held in trust for your children's lifetimes, allowing for payment of income, and have those assets distributed to your grandchildren on your children's death?

4. Do you have a disabled child? If yes, do you want to provide specially for that child? For example, do you want to take advantage of public assistance?

5. If in the unlikely event your spouse or domestic partner and all of your children and grandchildren are dead and no other disposition is made, to whom do you want to leave your property? Do you want to leave it all to your heirs? Do you want to leave it half to your heirs and half to your spouse or domestic partner's heirs? Everything to a charity or even to named individuals?

In this chapter, we have highlighted some basic planning techniques that you should be familiar with when planning for your family. This discussion of techniques is not exhaustive, however. The good news is that the number of planning alternatives that are available to you and your advisors is staggering. And so of course it is critical that you seek out professional planners to assist you in planning your FWPP.

9

DISINHERITING A SPOUSE OR DOMESTIC PARTNER

Do family members have rights?

The fundamental laws are in the long run merely statements that every event is itself and not some different event.

C. S. Lewis

In planning estates over the years I have often been asked, "What happens after my death if I want to disinherit my spouse or domestic partner?" And also, "If I do want to disinherit my spouse or domestic partner, can my spouse or domestic partner contest my will or trust and get my property?" The answer to both questions is that in Michigan disinherited spouses or domestic partners do have the right to receive some of the property that was not left to them.

Michigan law gives a surviving spouse or domestic partner the right to receive far less than half of the deceased spouse or domestic partner's property. The name the property is held in can become of critical importance on the death of a spouse or domestic partner, because in Michigan ownership rights not established during life will not be meaningfully restored automatically upon death. For example, in the past many couples were persuaded to leave up to one half of their property to their spouse or domestic partner in order to maximize federal estate tax savings. In the past, in order to qualify for the marital deduction/IRS grocery store double coupon day a surviving spouse or domestic partner had to be given at least the income from half of the deceased spouse or domestic partner's property and also the right to leave that property to anyone he or she chose. The requirements that a spouse or domestic partner had to be given the right to dispose of half the estate on his or her subsequent death of course brought about many tears and sometimes anger. Every spouse or domestic partner wanted to reduce federal estate tax, but many times preferred to give up the tax benefits of the near marital deduction-IRS grocery store double coupon day because they knew or suspected that half of their property would pass to their spouse or domestic partner's loved ones on the subsequent death. This was particularly true when each spouse or domestic partner had children from a prior marriage or when there were no children at all. It should come as no surprise that the typical "family" today is a blended family or a domestic partnership.

Under current laws your spouse or domestic partner no longer has to be given the right to leave half your property to whomever they want. The marital deduction/IRS grocery store double coupon day requirements now absolutely remove this prior planning impediment. However, if you are getting excited about the potential opportunity to disinherit your spouse or domestic partner and still obtain the federal estate tax savings resulting from the marital deduction/IRS grocery store double coupon day provisions of the federal estate tax laws, be careful. After your death your spouse or domestic partner will still have all the rights given under Michigan law to elect against your will and even against your trust.

If you choose to disinherit your spouse or domestic partner totally or partially, your estate planning needs can be determined only after you are aware of the rights afforded under Michigan law that are given to your spouse or domestic partner after your death. Knowledge of Michigan law will also enable you to better apply the techniques of planning that we discussed in Chapter 8, Planning for a Spouse or Domestic Partner. Two techniques are generally used to assure people that their spouse or domestic partner will not successfully elect against their will or trust. The first technique is called a prenuptial agreement. The second technique is called a post-nuptial agreement. A prenuptial agreement is used by persons who wish to marry but who also wish to establish their right to leave property to their loved ones prior to taking their marriage vows. Prenuptial agreements have been in use for a long time and are used more than ever today, particularly in second marriages. In order for these agreements to be valid, the following requirements usually must be met:

- Each party must be bound to the agreement and also consent to it.

- Each party must totally disclose all of their assets.

- The agreement must be in writing.

- Both parties must understand what they are signing.

Prenuptial agreements make it possible for spouse or domestic partners to protect the inheritance rights of their respective children from prior marriages and, as a result, prevent potential strife and stress over the disposition of their estates.

Postnuptial agreements, if they are properly prepared, can also set forth people's inheritance wishes. They are not legally recognized and enforced to the extent that prenuptial agreements are in Michigan. Michigan law is unique as it applies to post-nuptial agreements; it requires that they not only be negotiated in good faith and reduced to writing, but also there must be a complete and frank disclosure of all of the economic facts of each party to the other. The provisions, sometimes subject to court interpretation, must be "fair and reasonable." Lastly, all of the circumstances leading up to the signed agreement must be free from fraud, duress, and undue influence of any kind.

Postnuptial agreements are looked upon with suspicion by courts, and as a result, must be entered into very carefully. Because of this circumstance and the requirements for a postnuptial agreement, they are much more complicated and rigorous than a prenuptial agreement. Given a choice between signing a prenuptial agreement or a postnuptial agreement, always choose the former. They are much more easily enforced if they are valid, binding, fair, and fairly made at the time.

Second marriages offer the most troublesome of estate planning challenges. The trouble arises because many people have children from their prior marriage and want to assure that all or at least most of their estates go to those children. Alternatively, if there are children from one, two, or even three or more marriages, making sure all the children of the current spouse or domestic partner are all taken care of equitably and fairly can sometimes be very difficult. The best way to plan for a second marriage or more is through the use of a prenuptial agreement. Most problems concerning who gets what can be solved. If a prenuptial agreement was overlooked, perhaps a postnuptial agreement can also address and somewhat solve the problem.

What happens if neither a prenuptial agreement nor a postnuptial agreement can be used? Well, as you can imagine, the spouse or domestic partner in a second or third or more marriage also has rights. As a matter of fact, absent those agreements, their rights are exactly the same as the first spouse or domestic partner's rights given under Michigan law.

10

TRUSTEES—
MODERN SUPER HEROES

Wisdom and understanding can only become the possession of individual men by traveling the old road of observation, attention, perseverance, and industry.

Samuel Smiles

A trust-based plan requires three types of players: a trustmaker, trust beneficiaries, and the person who actually runs the trust: the trustee. Another great term for trustee is Hero, or better yet Superhero. Michigan law refers to these superheroes as fiduciaries, the word fiduciary being used interchangeably with trustee.

Trustees in General

When the trustee is named, that person is given, both by the trustmaker and by Michigan law, extensive rights and powers which are to be exercised on behalf of the trust beneficiaries. Trustees can be individual persons or properly professionally licensed state and federal institutions. Individual trustees are normally family members, friends, or other trusted advisors of the trustmaker. Institutional trustees include trust companies and the departments of commercial banks. These trustees are often referred to as corporate fiduciaries.

No matter who the trustee is, institutional or individual, they must act in a fiduciary capacity. When so acting, trustees have the ultimate duty imposed by law as to relationships between people. When trustees make mistakes and those mistakes are proven, they can be potentially liable to the beneficiaries for those mistakes. For a long time the trustee's actions and liability for those actions have been measured by what we refer to as "the reasonably prudent person rule." This rule basically asks the question, "Would a similar, reasonably prudent person acting in the same capacity in the same area and under the same or similar circumstances have made the same judgment?" If the answer to the question is no, trustees can be held liable for the consequences of their actions. The Michigan Trust Code further defines all of the various duties and responsibilities of trustees. There is also a recent trend to apply even tougher standards in the measurement of a trustee's actions. In Michigan, for example, the law has followed the trend in almost all of the other states and has adopted the Prudent Investor Rule. Under this rule, trustees must minimize the risk at any given level of return on trust assets. So, in effect, the prudent person rule has quickly become the prudent expert rule. Clearly, a prudent expert makes no mistakes at all—or so it would seem. We take no particular position on this trend; merely knowing it exists and is being amplified is enough.

Becoming, accepting, or naming a trustee is serious business. As previously stated, trustees are fiduciaries and of course then fiduciaries are superheroes and as superheroes are super liable for acts or failures to act that have not been super beneficial to sometimes what we refer to as not so super beneficiaries! Providing knowledge of the trustee's role and the consequences of poor performance in that role should prevent or limit kind but ill-prepared people from acting as trustees in the first place. You do not accommodate a family member, friend, or client by accepting a trusteeship without opening her eyes about what a trustee is and does. If you have volunteered to be a trustee, please re-examine and discuss your decision with whoever named you.

The trustee's role can be confusing. Trustees are totally responsible for expert performance and judgment while following the written instructions of the trustmaker for the benefit of the trustmaker's beneficiaries. They are also responsible, as experts, for the preservation of the trustmaker's property, its growth with respect to income and capital appreciation, and how that all applies to the beneficiaries.

People create relationships, and relationships in turn create people. Each and every relationship involves different expectations, duties, and results. Common sense tells us that most relationships are not fiduciary relationships; they are normally business or personal relationships. Laws have of course been created to govern these relationships, and all of them fall short of the excellence required under the current law.

Looking at this area with common sense reveals only two major responsibilities:

1. Trustees have an absolute mandate, by operation of law, to follow precisely the written instructions of the trustmaker.

2. Trustees have the absolute responsibility to read between the lines and make judgment calls when there is no clear cut alternative dictated by the trust agreement.

If the trustees are called upon to make decisions that are too difficult for them, they must ask a court to help them. This is particularly true in a family with dissension or in any type of controversial environment created by the beneficiaries or the trustmaker. Without further information, most clients view the trustee's role as primarily financial. After all, trustees are supposed to be financially astute; however not all trustees' decisions will be limited to financial areas. People decisions may affect the financial decisions. Thus our superhero needs to be not only super competent but supersensitive. It's difficult to find competent and willing trustees on both a personal and professional basis because trustees must work super hard and are always held super accountable for their hopefully super actions.

It should be obvious now that it's difficult to find competent and willing trustees on both a personal and an institutional basis because trustees must work super hard and are always super accountable for their actions. In discussing the selection of an appropriate trustee with our clients, most of the concerns center in the areas of the trustee's knowledge of their family's affairs, investment performance, and the empathy that will potentially be accorded to their beneficiaries. The trustee's knowledge of the affairs of the trustmaker is usually deficient. Our experience has shown that most people carry most of their affairs around in their heads. Most spouses, domestic partners, and children know too little if anything at all about the family's economic affairs. We believe that full disclosure is necessary, and you should brief your loved ones and anyone associated with your family regarding your financial affairs whenever possible and start now to communicate your affairs to the trustee.

Regarding investment performance, we often hear, "He wouldn't be very good, he can't even handle his own money," or "She certainly made a lot of money for herself—probably she'll do the right thing for me." How effective will he be in making the principal grow? What guarantees can I provide? There are no easy answers to these questions.

Trustees cannot speculate with principal or the income it generates. This does not mean that assets cannot be sold or traded, nor does it mean that trustees cannot invest in assets that could potentially go down in value. It does mean that trustees must make investments on a cautious basis. It also means that they must diversify, using good judgment in all cases, or perhaps even not diversify if the assets they are given are already profitable on a proven basis.

A trustee should not knowingly (if they're even aware of their liability) attempt to achieve a return predicated on a speculative investment. Trustee speculators are liable for those losses they create. Speculation with regard to one's own funds may be all right; if losses are incurred, they may be earned back through labor and industry. But if a trustee speculates and loses, that is not all right; if a trustee cannot pay back what they have lost, it probably cannot be replaced. The trustee's investment approach should always be cautious. It should be prudent and relatively risk-free. There's no room whatsoever for any kind of speculation in the assets contained in the portfolio managed by the trustee.

Conversely, trustees have been known to be too conservative in their investment strategies. The investment of funds at a below-market yield, in terms of both income and capital appreciation, can result in trustees being liable for lost opportunities. To act in a super way as it relates to super investments, it isn't necessarily safe to only use a prudent investment.

The accountability of trustees regarding their actions, thoughts, feelings, and relationships shown to the actual beneficiaries is difficult to ascertain and difficult to measure. Regardless of whether a professional or individual trustee is selected, there are no guarantees that sound overall investment performance will result or that the beneficiaries will be satisfied with the trustee. The point to remember is that trustees have awesome power, accountability, and liability all wrapped together in their roles as superheroes.

Institutional Versus Individual Trustees

How do institutional trustees measure up against individual trustees? Before answering this question, let's first outline the pros and cons as it relates to personal trustees. Obviously personal trustees are people. As such they have all of the normal human strengths and weaknesses we all have. A trustee can be you or others close to you. A brief job description of an ideal trustee would be an intelligent mature responsible person who knows and loves you. Here is a brief outline of the pros and cons attributed to different types of trustees.

Family Members

The pros of family members as trustees include knowledge of the family's personal investment and business affairs; they can be empathetic, loving and intelligent, have good common sense, and of course are personally involved in the family. The cons include being perhaps indecisive or insecure, having no track record or experience, being too emotionally involved, being unskilled at business, being prejudiced towards certain family members, and potentially being uncollectible if they make any mistakes.

Friend or Business Associate

The pros of a friend or business associate as trustee could include empathy, being a good business person, being a good personal investor, having good common sense, and being honest and hard-working. The cons include the fact that they are human, and as such they may embezzle, speculate poorly, or die. Another problem can be not having enough time, because this role can be a burden. They may play favorites either by default or by design. And in the event of a breach of their duties they are probably not very collectible.

Professional Advisors: Attorney, CPA, Financial Advisor

The pros of choosing a professional such as an attorney, CPA, or financial advisor to be a trustee include the fact that they are a trained professional, and may be honest, hard-working, and have a past history as a trusted advisor. The cons include the fact that, like the friend or business associate, professionals are also humans who can embezzle, speculate poorly, or die. The time burden can be especially acute for a professional; they may also play favorites; and, again, they're probably not very collectible.

The Institutional Trustee

The pros of an institutional trustee include the fact that they are of course a professional with experience and an established track record, and collectible in the event of a breach of their duties or bad work. Also in their favor is the fact that they will always be there and the fact that the bank doesn't move, get sick, or die. Additionally, the institutional trustee is not usually as emotionally involved as the others, consequently can be more objective, and is of course regulated by law. The cons include the possibility that they can be disinterested and/or ignorant of the family or its affairs. There is a somewhat high turnover among staff members at institutions, and they can be hard to reach, too conservative, or too slow to act.

The previous brief outline of the relative pros and cons of different types of trustees is obviously not all-inclusive. We are sure that you can add items to each and every category and we encourage you to do so.

Practical Advice on the Selection of Your Trustees

Our advice is that you should not pick a single trustee, whether an individual or an institution. It may be better to create combinations of trustees in your trust and provide a pattern for the succession of those trustees. Planning for the succession of trustees involves stating which trustees you want to take over in the event that the previous trustees quit, die, become disabled, or are fired. Providing for the selection of future trustees is good business. It can provide for the use of both personal and institutional trustees.

In your trust document, always spell out who has the authority to terminate a trustee. Trustees who are not doing the job to the satisfaction of the beneficiaries should be terminated. Many trusts we have reviewed do not provide for the termination of any trustees. We believe this is a big mistake. Poorly performing trustees who continue as trustees become a burden to the beneficiaries. They are not easy to get rid of unless the document provides for their termination.

The dilemma becomes that removing a trustee without specific termination or succession rights in the trust agreement itself requires the review and approval by a petition filed with a court of law. In Michigan that court is the local county's probate court. In our experience, using the court as a planning alternative is extremely poor, time-consuming, and expensive planning. There's absolutely no guarantee that the court will agree with the unhappy beneficiaries. And it goes without saying that the legal process is slow, expensive and normally produces disappointing results. The trustmaker should always stipulate in the agreement which beneficiaries may exercise the right to terminate the trustees. By so doing, hopefully we can eliminate the words that we never want to utter at our law firm, which are, of course, "Good morning, Your Honor!"

An important point to understand is that you should communicate your list of those individuals, and their succession, who are to have the power to fire the trustee at any time: and see that your instructions are clearly drafted into your trust agreement. Another major, and in our opinion mandatory, planning tool is for you to set forth who you want to take over as a trustee when a trustee is fired, quits, or dies. You can also provide for the appointment of trustees by giving others the right to select those trustees.

There is no limit to the personal and creative choices you can make; just make sure that you think about your choices clearly and see to it that your estate planner accomplishes your goals in this area. When naming the trustees for your trust, a good general rule could perhaps involve the idea of not naming your spouse or domestic partner as the sole trustee. It may make sense to give them some help. Based on counseling, if you desire you can name an adult child of yours, or if you prefer, all of your adult children. Perhaps you were closer to another family member, business associate, or advisor. If you are, and feel great about that person as a lifetime trusted advisor, you can name one or more of them as the trustee to act with your spouse or domestic partner. Again, just remember to provide for their determination and termination and replacement.

If your particular planning situation dictates that there are no personal trustee candidates to assist your spouse or domestic partner, perhaps you should select an institutional trustee. There is nothing wrong with naming an institution as a co-trustee. In fact, our experience suggests that some clients prefer this approach. If you decide to use this approach, always give your spouse or domestic partner the power to fire the institution and replace it according to their wishes and your instructions. You might want to combine the strengths of a personal trustee with the strengths of an institutional trustee. That way you may perhaps get the best of both worlds. Finally, your choice of trustee should also be based on your beliefs, values, and particular situation.

Trustee's Fees

"Does the trustee get paid?" "How much do they charge?" These are questions clients commonly ask. Yes, trustees have a right to be compensated. There is no such thing as a free lunch even in the trust business. Historically, trustees, especially professional trustees, charged an annual fee calculated as a percentage of the income earned by the trust property over the course of a year. This method is rarely used today.

Today most, if not all, institutional trustees charge and are paid pursuant to published fee schedules. The fee schedules generally are a percentage of the dollar value of the assets managed by the trustee. They are published to avoid any confusion that might otherwise arise between the trustee and the beneficiaries. The value the trustees apply their percentage fees to is the fair market value of the trust property as determined by the trustee. Institutional trustees almost always have a minimum fee that will be charged regardless of the value of the trust property. The minimum fee is not based on a percentage of assets, but is a fixed amount. Each institution, although independent, closely follows the structures of its competitors.

Reviewing the published fee schedules of institutional trustees suggests that they're all pretty much the same. Shopping for trustee's fees may not be very productive. Most if not all have a minimum fee and most use the percentage of value approach. The larger the institution, the more likely it will be to charge differently for extraordinary services. Some even have termination fees.

Personal or individual trustees are not as sophisticated of course in the manner in which they can or should charge fees. Many provide their services on a gratuitous or "act of love" basis. It's pretty rare that an individual or personal trustee would overcharge, but it does happen. Most of them in our opinion don't charge enough. The current standard under Michigan law is "a reasonable fee." If the trustee's fee is disputed by the beneficiaries, the matter has to be either negotiated or brought before the probate court, where a judge will ultimately settle the fee dispute based on the above standard. It's been our experience that trustee fees are not normally a major concern for most of our clients. The major concern for the majority if not all of our clients is how the trustee will perform their duties.

11

RETIREMENT PLANNING: GOOD PLANNING CREATES A GOOD LIFE

It is not the man who has too little,
but the man who craves more, that is poor.

Seneca

Congress has passed numerous laws allowing all kinds of retirement plans. There's a great deal of interest in retirement planning as America ages and the baby boomer generation begins to enter its golden years. Retirement plans have an enormous impact on FWPP. How they are planned for and structured during your lifetime and at your death can have significant income and estate tax consequences. So it's important to have at least a general understanding of the common types of retirement plans.

Types of Retirement Plans

There are a number of ways to classify retirement plans: employee-sponsored plans and individual plans; qualified and nonqualified plans; deferred compensation plans, stock bonus plans, stock option plans, and hybrid plans. We have found that the best way to understand the many types of plans is to begin with plans that are qualified under the Internal Revenue Code. Generally speaking, *qualified plans* are those plans that are governed and sanctioned by the Internal Revenue Code and that provide income tax incentives to employers and employees. These types of plans are generally instituted by employers for the benefit of their employees. The most common qualified plans are profit sharing plans, including 401(k) plans and money purchase pension plans. Each of these plans allows the employer to take an immediate income tax deduction for the amount of money paid into the plan. The employee does not have to take his or her share of the contribution of money into income tax consideration until they have the right to share it and actually take it out of the plan.

Within the categories of all qualified plans, there are specific types of plans. For example, employee stock ownership plans, ESOPs, are allowed to hold the stock of the sponsoring company. Other examples of qualified plans are savings incentive match plans for employees (SIMPLE plans), and employee pension plans (SEPs). Qualified plans are required to cover most of the employees in a business. There are very complicated rules about who must be allowed to participate in these plans. These rules also make sure that employees are vested in the plans over a relatively short period of time. The rules may require that the plan be subject to strict funding rules and that the plan be insured by an agency of the federal government.

Individual retirement accounts, IRAs, are not qualified plans. They are individual plans. In fact, IRAs are covered under separate sections of the Internal Revenue Code and are not part of ERISA, the law that governs all qualified plans. (At the law firm we affectionately refer to this federal law as "Every Ridiculous Idea Since Adam.")

Some companies sponsor IRA plans, but IRAs are not designed as compensation plans for businesses; they are savings plans. Contributions to these types of plans are made directly by the participant, not by the employer. There are rules as to who can contribute to these plans and how much of the contribution is tax-deductible. The tax-deductible amount that can be contributed to an IRA is far less than the maximum contributions allowed in other qualified plans.

Some retirement plans are not qualified. For the most part, the non-qualified plan is one for which a company cannot take an immediate income tax deduction. On the employee side, a non-qualified plan is usually one in which the company promises to make certain payments in the future.

A typical non-qualified plan is a deferred compensation plan. In these plans, the company promises to pay compensation to the employee at some point in the future, usually at retirement. There is no assurance whatsoever that the money will ever be paid, other than the company's promise. Payments are not deductible to the company until paid. Likewise, the employee does not take the payments into consideration for income tax purposes until they are actually received.

Non-qualified plans do not have to cover all employees in a company and are almost always reserved for only a few employees. Sometimes these plans are funded by life insurance or by a pool of money that is set aside for the future payments. The funds that are set aside, including life insurance contracts, must be subject to the claims of the company's creditors. That is why when the funds are set aside for the employees, they do not have to be included as income. If the company offered a non-qualified plan that actually set aside money in a way that the company's creditors could access, then the employees would have to take those amounts into immediate income tax consideration. Because non-qualified plans are mere promises to pay rather than separately funded plans, employees are concerned about whether the money will be available when they actually retire. Methods have been invented to separate the funds while not making them so separate and segregated as to avoid the creditors of the company. One method that is used to separate the funds is life insurance. Typically, the company purchases a cash value life insurance policy on the life of the employee. The company is both the owner and the beneficiary of the policy. Then when the employee retires, the company merely borrows funds from the policy to pay the deferred compensation that is owed to the employee at that time. If the employee dies during the period when he or she is being paid, then the death proceeds are used to pay off the remainder of the payments. If the employee dies before retirement, all or part of the death proceeds are paid to their family, trust, or estate. In all cases, when the funds are paid as part of compensation, they are deductible to the company and they are considered income to the recipient.

Estate Tax Impact of Retirement Plans

In a few exceptions, both qualified and non-qualified retirement plans can have substantial negative FWPP consequences. Any time retirement funds are paid after the death of the plan participant, at least two taxes apply: both the federal estate tax and the federal income tax. The full value of qualified retirement plans, including IRAs, is considered to be part of the participant's estate. The only exception to this rule is for pension plans that terminate on the death of the participant. For many reasons, it is impractical for a person to give away a qualified plan to another person during their lifetime or maybe even after their death. Because non-qualified plans are not controlled by the same laws as qualified plans, it is possible to remove the proceeds from the estate of the employee with good, forward-thinking planning.

Let's take a look at what it means to have the value of the plan included in the participant's estate. First, if the participant's spouse or domestic partner is the beneficiary of the plan, the value of the plan will be subject to the unlimited marital deduction. So, using the IRS double coupon, no estate tax will be due regardless of the size of the plan when the participant dies, so long as the spouse or domestic partner is the beneficiary. When the spouse or domestic partner dies, the full remaining value of the plan, if any, will be included in his or her estate.

Income Tax Impact of Retirement Plans

The technical term given by the IRS to income that is earned by a decedent before his or her death, but paid after death, is income in respect of a decedent (IRD). Special income tax rules are associated with IRD; none of them are very friendly. Expecting the IRS to be friendly to you because you are a taxpayer is like expecting a grizzly bear not to attack you because you're a vegetarian. Not only is IRD included in the estate of the decedent, but the proceeds are also subject to income tax when they are received by the beneficiary. Yes, you read that right. IRD is taxed at least twice, once under the estate tax rules and once again under the income tax rules.

An exception to the income tax results of IRAs is the Roth IRA. The proceeds from the Roth IRA are not subject to income tax, but they are subject to estate tax. For purposes of FWPP and income tax planning, a Roth IRA is generally superior to a standard IRA.

Retirement Planning Alternatives

Because of the nature of IRD, there are few retirement plan alternatives that will substantially reduce both income and estate tax consequences. However, there are a few alternatives that may perhaps work for you. For those who have very large IRAs or qualified plans that will be subject to both income and estate tax, the first step is to understand that eventually any funds left in those plans will be subject to taxes. Once that fact is digested, then the decision has to be made as to what impact that will have on your estate. Some people come to the conclusion that it's better to give the proceeds to charity than to see a vast majority of the fund go to taxes. These people, if married, name their spouse, domestic partner, or revocable living trust as the primary beneficiary of their plan because of the IRS double coupon. After the death of the spouse or domestic partner, their plan names a favorite charity or charities as the fund beneficiary. If a charity is the beneficiary, the money passes directly to the charity without being subject to reduction from taxes. Because in some cases much of it would pass to the government otherwise, this at least allows people to control how the proceeds will be used in the event there's anything left.

The second solution is to create an irrevocable life insurance trust (ILIT) and fund it with enough life insurance to pay the taxes on the retirement plan. The ILIT proceeds are not subject to federal estate tax, so they can be fully used to pay all state and income taxes on the retirement plan proceeds. ILITs are also used when the proceeds of the plan are paid to charity; life insurance proceeds are used to replace the retirement plan proceeds.

The retirement plan itself can be the source of the premium payments for the ILIT, even though after-tax dollars are used. Because a majority of funds in the retirement plan could be lost to income and estate taxes anyway, plan participants should not avoid taking money out of the plan and buying life insurance to protect or replace the retirement plan proceeds. While buying life insurance as a protection for errors is not always the most efficient use of funds, in the majority of cases it can nevertheless be well advised and implemented.

ILITs can also be used to fund the taxes on non-qualified retirement plans. Because the proceeds from these plans are also IRD and subject to the state income tax, an ILIT can be a source of tax-free cash to pay the taxes generated by the non-qualified deferred compensation payments.

Finally, some financial planners have taken the view that it is better not to touch the retirement plan proceeds for as long as possible. When forced to take the proceeds, they suggest that you take out only the minimum amounts. The rationale behind this concept is that by growing the retirement funds on a tax-deferred basis and then delaying the payment of taxes for as long as possible, even after the taxes are taken out more assets will be available to pass on to your heirs. The basic rule in this area seems to be the famous three-D's of tax planning: defer-defer-defer.

Perhaps deferral will create a better tax result; but you should be careful of the assumptions that are being made. Because of the complexity of the rules surrounding retirement planning, it is important to read and study this area as much as you possibly can. We then advise that you consult with counseling oriented planning partners who will rationally and patiently explain all of the available alternatives. In our view, retirement planning is not planning at all unless you have a clear goal in mind. Many times, tax savings are not of the greatest concern to families. Other factors and personal goals such as health, family dynamics, and the availability of assets outside of the retirement plan all influence the type of planning that is appropriate. We like to say that sometimes it's not proper to allow the tax tail to wag the planning dog.

In the end, it's your chance to save, spend, pass along, give away, or leave your money to charity. With a trusted, competent, experienced financial advisor and a love for yourself and your family, a lot of this can be planned for.

12

LIVE TOO LONG OR DIE TOO SOON[5]

The Longer You Live, The Longer You Live— But Once You're Dead— You're Dead

L et's get right to the point. What is your money really doing for you? Did you ever say to yourself, "Someday when I have more money, I'll…"? Have you actually done all the things you always wanted to do? Are you doing what you want to do now? Are you spending your time, talents and resources doing what you really want to do? What are your goals? If you could have the perfect situation, what would it be?

---

5 *This chapter contains information and cartoons from* The Wright Exit Strategy *by Bruce Raymond Wright.*

These are the questions I ask all of my clients in order to achieve clarity about their vision for life, business and finances. Getting a concise, articulate list of goals usually requires a lot more probing on my part, however. Most often the answers to these questions are tangled in an individual's perception of how things currently are. When setting goals, people are often influenced by other people's opinions, or limited by what they think they already know about money, taxes, etc. For example, many people tell me they would love to sell a problematic building or stock. But then they say, "The capital gains taxes ares so high I just can't sell it." They don't know there are several tactics they could implement to eliminate the capital gains tax on the sale of such assets. A person's lack of knowledge or misconception of technical issues often limits that person's options. Such self-limitation must be overcome if optimum results are to be achieved.

We are all trapped by our limited knowledge. It is this limitation which ultimately interferes with our ability to achieve wide-angle macro vision, to dream, set goals or move ahead. When clients say they cannot sell an appreciated asset without paying capital gains taxes, I could immediately jump into a teacher mode and explain various techniques for avoiding the payment of capital gains taxes. However, it is more helpful to stay focused on defining the vision and then explain the various techniques or tactics after all of the goals are identified. It took me a while to figure this out. Crystal clear vision and goal definition are so important that they must come first. If we cannot articulate and stand by our vision and goals, we become moving targets. No one can help us, and we cannot help ourselves if we keep changing our mind or redefining our goals. It is crucial that we devote the necessary time to establish goals which are true to our wide-angle vision and to what we ultimately desire so that we can stick to them. When developing goals, remember that you can still build in enough flexibility to allow for changes and your own evolution.

So just how can we work together to overcome the many obstacles that would interfere with our vision and goal-setting process? It's really rather simple; it can be summed up with this question: "If you could wave a magic wand and completely ignore the tax and investment laws, or your perception of them, what would your perfect situation be?" We need to free ourselves of our misconceptions and ignore what we think we know, and concentrate on what we really want.

We also need to make sure that we are actually setting goals and not just focusing on strategies. Using football as a metaphor, the football team enters the field; their goal is to win the game. However, there may be several strategies they can employ to achieve that goal depending on the strengths and weaknesses of the team, their opponent, and the circumstances. The goal or objective is the desired end result: to win. The strategy and tactics are the means used to achieve the goal. The same is true in the FWPP game. Strategies available to help keep your wealth will be fulfilled through a variety of tactics—trusts, partnerships, foundations, etc. However, when setting financial lifestyle goals, many people forget to concentrate on the goals and spend too much time concentrating on the strategies, or worse, the tools. It's literally the difference between clarity and certainty. You can be very clear about your goals, like the football team, about the play you are going to run and everyone's role or job within the play. However you can't be certain about the outcome—a touchdown. The point is, more clarity tends to lead to more certainty. As you might imagine, we have encountered many different personalities, perceptions, and paradigms. We have seen our clients utilize a variety of methods and mechanisms to build their estates and accumulate wealth. We have come to understand it takes a certain focus and mindset to accumulate wealth and build an estate. However, it requires a much different focus and approach to plan, protect, preserve, and make the most of your wealth once you've earned it. You can be extremely effective at earning money and increasing your net worth only to find yourself empty-handed because you failed to manage your wealth and avoid various pitfalls.

What pitfalls am I talking about? Changing economic or market conditions,capital gains taxes, income and excise taxes, estate taxes, litigation, changing laws, inaccurate or incompetent advice, failure to act upon good advice, and many other financial pitfalls can rob you of your wealth. How many times have you seen celebrities or professional athletes in the news who have lost significant fortunes because they have put their trust in dishonest or incompetent people or failed to manage or truly diversify their wealth effectively? One of the wealth advisors I work with likes to use the metaphor of the hot air balloon. As the balloon fills with air, the yellow, red and blue silks expand. The balloon begins to rise above the ground, heading for beautiful skies. Just as the balloon is about to escape gravity's hold, it is yanked to a stop. Tethered to the ground by ropes, the balloon is unable to free itself.

That hot air balloon is you and everyone who wants to make the most of their wealth. Your wealth is the hot air which should enable you to rise and reach your goals; however, there are ropes attached that may prevent you from reaching your true goal—freedom. These ropes are different for everyone. See if any of these common restraints are pulling on you and holding you down:

- Conflicting advice or information from different sources.
- Too much or too little information.
- Waiting for the tax laws to change.
- Rental property headaches.
- Decline in real estate or other asset value.
- Interest rate fluctuations.
- Rising costs.
- Heirs worried that you might jeopardize their inheritance.
- Retirement options and indecision.
- Procrastination when making necessary changes.
- Fear of making any changes at all.
- The list goes on...

Then there is that huge rope attached to your balloon called Congress. I'm sure it comes as no surprise at all that the "boys and girls along the Potomac" want a huge piece of your estate now while you're alive and again after you die. Income taxes, capital gains taxes, excise and estate taxes, and many other tax issues are pulling on you. Some of them may be holding you down, preventing you from reaching new heights and going where you want to go.

There is an old tale from India about a wise Rajah who wanted to study an important aspect of human nature. The Rajah gathered six blind gurus together and asked them to define a creature by touch. Because all the gurus were blind since birth, they had never seen such a creature. To make certain the gurus would not be prejudiced by previous descriptions they may have heard, they were not told what kind of animal it was.

Each blind guru was assigned to a different part of the creature and allowed to touch only that portion of the animal to which he was assigned. The first guru touched the tusk and said, "This animal is like a spear." The second guru felt the trunk and declared, "This animal is like a snake." Feeling the ear, the third guru exclaimed, "This animal is like a fan." The fourth guru touched the creature's front leg and announced, "This animal is like a tree." The fifth guru after patting the creature's side declared, "This animal is like a wall." Finally, the sixth guru grasped the tail and proclaimed, "This animal is like a rope."

The six blind gurus began arguing over who was right and who was wrong. Because each of these gurus had an ego and pride, as most of us do, the argument became quite heated. At this point, the wise Rajah who had set up the contest stepped in and said, "The elephant is a large animal, made up of different parts. Each of you has knowledge of only one part. To find out the whole truth, you must gain knowledge of all the parts and put them altogether. In order to do this, you must set aside your ego and pride to realize you may not have all the knowledge necessary to comprehend the whole elephant." This story exemplifies the essence of macro or big picture thinking.

We need to learn to see the whole elephant.

In some ways, we can all be like the blind gurus. Trying to get an accurate perspective or find the truth in life, finances, etc., can be very difficult, especially if we are too close to the situation. The most accurate and helpful knowledge is often gained when we step back from the situation and try to look at it from more angles. In order to do this effectively, we often need to have help from several sources and for several reasons. First if it is about *us* or *our* personal situation, the closer we are to an issue, the more emotional we tend to be. The more emotional we become, the less objective we are. Secondly, we cannot be experts in everything important to our success. We don't know what all the angles are or everything to look for. Thus, we often need third-party help to accurately perceive and overcome obstacles or to take advantage of opportunities.

When we're introduced to new clients, the conversation usually begins with a very particular problem to solve. People tend to focus on one specific issue, not the whole picture. They want to know how to fix that prominent problem now, yet rarely is it in someone's best interest to proceed with solutions at this point in time. Many people don't realize that every action they take concerning their assets may very well impact their entire net worth. Therefore, it is critical that we have a clear understanding of the whole "elephant," the complete financial and personal long-term vision and goals, before we undertake any critical changes. It's even safer to say, before we undertake any changes, most people do not know enough about financial issues, tax issues, etc., to differentiate what is critical and what is not, and what all of the ramifications might be.

The most common definition of estate planning that we have heard around the country is, "When you're dead, how are we going to divide up your stuff?" That's Level I estate planning. Level II is, "How do you generate maximum living benefits from your estate during your lifetime, and then how do you most effectively distribute your estate to your heirs or charitable causes after you pass away?" This is a better approach than Level I, but there is a higher level, Level III. Level III is where true big picture legacy and wealth planning actually takes place.

Level III asks, "What is your 100-year plan? What are you going to do while you are alive to fulfill your 100-year plan, and how will your vision and goals be carried out after you're gone?"

This holistic approach requires much more than just taking care of yourself now and distributing money later to your heirs. With a 100-year plan, you are creating a legacy while you are alive and furthering that legacy after you are gone. If you are over sixty years of age, you may think that a 100-year plan doesn't make any sense for you, but it really does. If you and your heirs can adopt and live this 100-year philosophy of life, how much more effective will you be than those who live in a day-to-day, moment-to-moment, rudimentary existence? We had one client who is in his late seventies say to us, "I don't even buy green bananas anymore, because that's how long-term my thinking is. How on earth can I get motivated to set up a 100-year plan?" Establishing a 100-year plan is not an easy task, but then almost nothing worthwhile or of real value is perceived as easy. However, if you follow five basic steps, your own 100-year plan will become a reality:

1. Gather and internalize information about true, personal, holistic goal setting.

2. Establish written vision and goals.

3. Create and draft a plan.

4. Implement the plan.

5. Revise and review at least every two years.

Sometimes our dilemma as advisors is that some clients just won't let us help them as exemplified in the cartoon below.

An important observation: Even the greatest teachers cannot teach an unwilling student.

The most effective advisors know they can only help clients who are willing to replace ambiguity with crystal clear vision. Being clear about your vision and what your best interests are gives advisors the clarity they need to protect, serve and further your best interests. Committed to writing and broken down into manageable goals, strategies, tactics, tools, time-lines and benchmarks, you will have a written plan. Such a plan not only provides clarity of purpose and how you will achieve what you want, it also assigns accountability and responsibility to succeed.

13

LIFE INSURANCE

You Are Blessed— FWPP Rocket Fuel

And that's the way it is...

Walter Cronkite

L ife insurance is generally purchased to satisfy one of two FWPP objectives: to create an estate or to protect an estate that has already been created. This chapter presents some ideas on how life insurance should be purchased to protect an estate that has already been built. Currently, most planning for U.S. citizens' surviving spouses or domestic partners and other family members will result in no tax liability on the death of the first spouse or domestic partner. This is true regardless of the size of the estate. The tax bite may perhaps be deferred and delayed to the second spouse or domestic partner's death.

Many existing life insurance policies insure the life of the primary wage earner. Sometimes life insurance is purchased to make sure there's enough income if the wage earner dies. It is purchased long before there is ever a FWPP problem and it ends up being used, perhaps, to pay for the federal estate tax, if any. In larger estates, life insurance is actually purchased in anticipation of paying the federal estate taxes, with no thought ever given to the tax effects do the cost of the insurance in the first place. Actuarially, age and gender do not make much difference any more. Historically it was more expensive to insure the male if he was the older of the two, because statistically males tended to die younger than females. That is no longer the case. If the male dies first, the purpose for which the insurance was purchased may not even materialize. The bottom line with regard to life insurance for most FWPP tax planning is this: do not just insure a spouse or partner based on reasons related to the first death; rather insure for both the first and the second death, which is when the taxes and most replacement income will be needed or incurred. Insuring only a second death also presents another problem: how can you and your advisors know with certainty in what sequence the deaths will occur? Obviously, there can be no precise answer to this question. What can be determined, however, is whether you or your spouse or domestic partner are less expensive to insure right now. An insurance company will be happy to tell you this.

If your spouse or partner is less expensive to insure than you are, why not insure their life rather than yours? If you as the older spouse or partner fulfill the actuarial role and die first, there will be no federal estate tax and no need for life insurance proceeds to pay that tax. On your spouse or partner's subsequent death, there may be taxes, and the insurance proceeds will be there.

If your spouse or partner dies first, there will be no taxes but there will be the proceeds from the insurance. Those proceeds could be invested in liquid assets to assist with living expenses. Upon your death, funds would be available to pay taxes or pass on to other beneficiaries and heirs. In either case, regardless of the sequence of death, insuring the younger spouse or partner can save significant premium dollars. Regardless of whose life is insured, the proceeds can be available to pay taxes resulting from the death of the surviving spouse or partner. Many insurance companies provide a unique product called a joint-and-survivor policy or a second-to-die policy. This type of policy insures two lives and pays out death proceeds only on the death of the second to die. If your total amount of assets are greater than the IRS double coupon, this is a method for ensuring the payment of the potential death taxes. Joint and survivor policies have merit. However, if the life insurance proceeds are needed for any other purpose, insuring the younger spouse or partner may be the better alternative. The decision as to whether to insure the younger of the two or to purchase a joint-and-survivor policy can generally be reduced to an economic decision based on the relative premium costs of each product.

In our experience, different companies have different premium structures for each of their various insurance products. An experienced, intelligent, trusted advisor should be able to generate a comparison between all of the alternatives and the various costs associated with implementing each choice.

The decision between these two products may not entirely hinge on economics. There may be many couples who will elect to insure the younger spouse or partner rather than purchase the joint-and-survivor policy just in case the younger spouse or partner does the unexpected and dies first. If the younger spouse or partner does die first, the other spouse or partner will have the insurance proceeds to use and invest during their lifetime.

Please remember that this discussion applies only to life insurance purchased solely to protect an estate already created. One question that will certainly surface as a result of our discussion in this area is, "Can I afford to cash in existing policies that I've been paying on for years?" We do not recommend that existing policies be canceled or terminated or cashed in until two steps are accomplished under the direction of your financial advisor or insurance professional:

1. Make a complete analysis of the relative costs between existing policies and new policies.

2. If the new method is truly less expensive, old policies should still not be canceled or cashed in until the new policies are actually in force. Too many clients have made this mistake and then found out that they were uninsurable or insurable only at very high cost because of health problems.

We know that the insurance industry has gone through a rate and premiums revolution recently, and from what we see, this trend is continuing. People are living longer and remaining healthier longer. As a result of low interest rates and a host of other economic factors, insurance rates and the amount of coverage available for your premium dollar have been in harmonious relationship with each other. We have been relatively astounded at the rates many of the insurance professionals we have worked with have been able to quote for our clients. We were also astounded at the number of new policy formats and techniques and tools recently introduced into the marketplace as it relates to the wide variety of insurance products, including some features related to disability. The standing rule that someone should never cancel a policy that has been in existence for some period of years no longer seems to be a good rule. As always we encourage you to seek out the advice and counsel of a genuinely interested, intelligent and competent insurance professional to determine and perhaps redetermine whether or not your insurance portfolio is properly structured.

14

THE IRREVOCABLE LIFE INSURANCE TRUST

"Let Them Eat Cake"

The race is not to the swift or the battle to the strong...but time and chance happen to them all.

Ecclesiastes 9:11

As we have said, life insurance proceeds provide the fuel that powers many an FWPP car; however, most of the time, the fuel mixture is taxed at the pump before it finds its way into the vehicle. A disadvantage generally associated with the purchase of life insurance is that those proceeds usually increase the taxable estate of the policy owner. On the death of an insured owner, the life insurance proceeds are included in the insured owner's estate for federal estate tax purposes. Most people buy life insurance with the belief that those proceeds can be used by their beneficiaries free of tax. If the insured owns a policy on his or her own life, all of the insurance proceeds are includable in his or her estate for federal estate tax.

In order to avoid federal estate tax, many people have life insurance on their lives owned by their spouses, partners, or others so that upon the death of the insured, the policy proceeds are paid to the owner's beneficiary, free of federal estate tax.

There are problems associated with the cross-ownership technique:

- The insured loses control of the life insurance policies.

- Proceeds are usually taxed on the death of the policy-owner if he or she is the beneficiary and dies after the insured.

- Few people can plan for the contingency that the owner-beneficiary may in fact die first.

- If the proceeds are payable to someone other than the insured or the owner, there is a gift of the entire insurance proceeds to the beneficiary from the policy-owner. The goal sought by insurance policy cross-ownership is a noble one. However, there's a better way to accomplish this goal. You can use an irrevocable life insurance trust (ILIT) to own life insurance policies that insure your life. By using an ILIT, the insurance proceeds will be free of federal estate tax upon your death. In addition, if you plan for your spouse or partner, the ILIT will keep the proceeds out of their estate as well.

The ILIT has been used as an FWPP technique since federal estate tax laws were implemented. These trusts were designed to keep life insurance proceeds free of federal estate tax. Because the government was losing tax revenue, the Internal Revenue Service, of course, attacked their use on many grounds and as a result the ILIT temporarily fell into disuse. However, today they are frequently used and, quite frankly, are enjoying a heyday. Once you understand how the ILIT works you will appreciate why they're so popular. Generally, if a life insurance policy is given away, the value of the life insurance proceeds will not be included in the estate of the person who gave the policy away. Whoever gives a life insurance policy away must be careful not to retain incidents of ownership in the policy. This means that the person who gives a policy away must not retain control over the use of the life insurance policy in any way.

The ILIT is used to own an insurance policy, whether it is purchased by the ILIT or given to it. The ILIT, as its name implies, must be irrevocable. Once the trust is drafted and signed, it can never be changed, except by the courts and then only under very special circumstances. If an ILIT is not totally irrevocable or if the trustmaker retains strict control over it, the insurance proceeds will not be free of federal estate tax.

Using an ILIT, three estate planning objectives can be achieved:

- Insurance proceeds can be kept free of federal estate tax upon the death of both spouses or partners.

- Because of the terms provided in the trust document the trustmaker can control the insurance proceeds received by the ILIT to care for the trustmaker's beneficiaries.

- The life insurance proceeds received by an ILIT can be used to pay the death expenses, including taxes, of both the trustmaker and the trustmaker's spouse or partner.

The beneficiaries of an ILIT are generally exactly the same as the beneficiaries of the trustmaker's revocable living trust. In fact, the terms of the ILIT give the value of the existing policy and design according to the advice and counsel of your insurance planning professional.

You can transfer your existing policies into your ILIT, or you can have your ILIT purchase brand-new insurance policies on your life. The latter is easier. Through gifts of cash from you or others, the ILIT receives funds so that it can pay premiums on life insurance policies it owns on your life, or it can pay those premiums from income generated by other property you have transferred into your ILIT. In order to make this succeed, the federal gift tax consequences of these transfers must be examined.

The current annual exclusion for gifts is $14,000, indexed for inflation. The annual exclusion can be used only when there is a gift of a present interest in property. A present interest is a gift of which the recipient can have both the current use and benefit of the gift. A gift of a life insurance policy or the money to pay its premiums is generally not a gift of a present interest when given to a trust. If there were no annual exclusion available for life insurance, the use of an ILIT might not be attractive, but this apparent problem has been solved. A man named Mr. Clifford Crummey established a special irrevocable trust for the benefit of his beneficiaries. Under his trust, his beneficiaries were to receive property from the trust sometime in the future. Mr. Crummey deducted the annual exclusion for the gifts he made to his trust and of course, the IRS took him to court. Mr. Crummey beat the court and he beat the IRS.

Mr. Crummey won because his irrevocable trust had an added feature. This feature is called a demand right, which is simply the ability of the beneficiary, for a limited period of time, to ask for and receive from the trust the value of the current gifts made to the trust. Because of the demand right, a present interest is created in the property given to the ILIT, and the annual exclusion is available. Because of Mr. Crummey, your gifts to your ILIT can qualify for the federal gift tax annual exclusion

There may be a practical problem with giving others such a demand right. The beneficiaries may demand their share of the premium money; however, in our experience, this has not been a problem. The right is refused by beneficiaries and the money is used to pay the life insurance premiums. After all, the beneficiaries are normally your family members, and even though they are free to exercise their rights, they will likely understand that by not exercising them they will be helping the family's overall tax situation and of course will ultimately receive the money anyway.

There are some income tax ramifications of trusts, many of which affect the ILIT. For example, if you name your spouse or partner as trustee or beneficiary of your ILIT, any income that the trust generates will be taxed to you. Usually, this does not present a problem, because in ILIT is generally not designed to create any taxable income. However, this provision, as well as others, may have an effect on your planning. The income tax issues alone of an ILIT provide a good reason to check with an experienced professional before establishing an ILIT.

Having a friendly trustee is important. Second reading of Chapter 10 is probably a good idea. The trustees and their successors must be provided for in the original ILIT trust document.

There is one more pitfall in giving life insurance policies to an ILIT. If a life insurance policy is given to your ILIT within three years of the date of your death, the life insurance proceeds are brought back into your estate for federal estate tax purposes. This could also be true for insurance policies purchased directly by your ILIT. Therefore, it is best for the trustee to apply for the life insurance policy as the owner, to reduce the risk that the insurance policies will be included in your estate if you die within three years after the date of the insurance policy becoming effective.

Almost any type of insurance can be used in an ILIT. Term, whole life, universal life, universal variable life, or corporate insurance, properly structured, can all be used.

Creating an ILIT that will meet your objectives and will really work when you need it to work requires the hands of both an expert FWPP attorney and an expert insurance professional. To use less than the best is to invite disaster. As we have stated throughout this book, if you use competent, intelligent, counseling-oriented planning partners, your ILIT will allow you to have your cake and eat it too.

PART IV

THE OTHER ONE DIES

15

THE TAX MAN COMETH

Surprise Surprise—
He Looks Like Darth Vader!

The sky is not less blue because
the blind man does not see it.

Danish Proverb

Transfer/Death Taxes

The American Taxpayer Relief Act (ATRA) is the most significant legislation impacting the federal transfer tax system since 2001. ATRA permanently establishes the estate tax exemption amount—the IRS Grocery Store coupon—at $5,000,000 per person, annually adjusted for inflation. From our perspective as a planner, there is some comfort in the fact that ATRA has made these changes permanent. That is, unlike past legislation there are no sunset provisions in the new legislation. Given the current budgetary climate, however, time will tell whether any such comfort is short-lived. Another significant development was the United States Supreme Court decision in the case of United States versus Windsor in 2013, in which the court ruled that section 3 of the Defense of Marriage Act was unconstitutional as applied to persons of the same sex who were legally married under the laws of their state, because it violated the Equal Protection Clause of the Fifth Amendment to the U.S. Constitution. Following this decision the IRS issued guidance concluding that, for federal death tax purposes, same-sex couples will be treated as married if they are legally married in a jurisdiction that recognizes same-sex marriages, even if they live in or move to a jurisdiction that does not.

More recently the United States Supreme Court has ruled in the case of Obergefell vs Hodges. Consequently, same-sex married couples may take advantage of the same benefits previously enjoyed only by opposite-sex married couples.

The Federal Tax System

The federal transfer or death tax system, which is part of the Internal Revenue Code, imposes taxes on the gratuitous transfer of property. The system has three components; the estate tax, the gift tax, and the generation-skipping tax (GST). To ensure transfer taxation at every generational level, the GST was enacted. Before the adoption of the GST tax, it was possible for a person to leave property in trust for the benefit of their children for their children's lifetimes. The property in the trust would then pass to the person's grandchildren without any transfer taxation at the children's generation. Under the existing GST tax scheme, the transfer to the grandchildren would not be subject to estate tax in the child's estate but would be subject to the GST tax if it was not exempt.

Fortunately, Michigan has repealed its inheritance tax. Effective for people who die after September 30, 1993, this tax was replaced by the "soak up" or "pick up" tax. At this time there is no Michigan estate, GST, or inheritance tax.

There is one area in which the federal government has failed to adopt a workable tax: capital gain taxes on a deceased person's appreciated assets. For example, if a taxpayer owns an asset purchased for $100 but later sold for $1000, the taxpayer recognizes a gain of $900. This transaction is subject to income tax as a long-term capital gain. If the taxpayer sells the asset during his or her lifetime the capital gains taxes paid on the balance of the proceeds are includable in the taxpayer's estate.

If by chance the taxpayer were to die before selling the asset, the asset would be included in the taxpayer's estate at its full fair market value of $1000. If the estate, or the beneficiary who receives the asset, later sells it for $1000, there is no capital gains tax to pay. In other words, the $900 of gain would never be subject to income tax. The asset gets a new cost basis, often referred to as a "stepped-up" basis, namely, the full fair market value of the asset as of the date of death.

No discussion of the transfer or death taxes would be complete without a brief discussion of valuation. Valuation is currently the most prevalent issue in the area of estate and gift tax audits. It's also one of the most difficult issues to resolve. Assets are valued for federal transfer or death tax purposes at fair market value. Some assets are easy to value: cash, publicly traded securities, and life insurance. Other assets are more difficult to value, such as real estate and securities that are not publicly traded.

For FWPP planning purposes, it is sufficient to use twice the state equalized value for residential real estate in Michigan. That being said, currently the Internal Revenue Service has indicated it will not accept twice the state equalized value for gift and estate tax purposes. For real estate, the first choice for evaluation is an appraisal by a qualified appraiser. Real estate used for farming or in a trade or business may qualify for special valuation rules for these purposes if the estate qualifies and the personal representative makes the appropriate election, which is often not understood and overlooked.

It's interesting that unlike what most people would assume, the book value of an operating business is not a reliable valuation method. However, in an entity that does not conduct an active business, such as a holding company consisting of publicly traded stocks, it may be possible to value the entity based on the underlying fair market value of both the assets and liabilities. At one time, a portion of the value of a qualified family-owned business could qualify for a deduction for estate tax purposes but not for gift tax purposes. However, this is no longer the case since its repeal in 2012.

For estate tax purposes, be sure to use the face value of life insurance instead of the cash surrender value. For gift tax purposes the value of the whole life policy that has been in force for some time and is not paid up must be analyzed professionally to ensure that the correct value is being used. As you begin your FWPP process, estimates of value of your assets are fine. This will allow the planner to determine if the net worth of a particular client for estate tax purposes is below, at, or above the threshold for federal estate taxation.

Federal Estate and Gift Taxes—Common Elements

ATRA has also made permanent the portability of the estate tax exemption. (You can give the unused part of your IRS grocery store coupon to your spouse.) Essentially, if an individual dies and leaves any of his or her IRS grocery store coupon unused, the surviving spouse will be able to add that unused amount to his or her own coupon. In order to make use of this unused portion of the coupon, the estate must prepare and file a federal estate tax return.

Applicable Exclusion Amount—IRS Grocery Store Coupon

Before 1977, the Internal Revenue Code provided for an exemption of a certain amount of property. In 1976, the exemption was repealed and replaced with a credit against tax, which was called the unified credit. Congress tinkered with the tax again in 1997 and increased the credit and changed the terminology; however, the statutory language referred to the applicable credit amount. In addition, there was no stated dollar amount of the credit in the statute. Instead, the statute referred to a specific exemption amount called the applicable exclusion amount, which throughout this book we have referred to as the IRS grocery store coupon. The coupon is available against taxable gifts made during the client's lifetime, and the balance of the coupon, if any, is available to use at death.

Each person—for gift tax purposes—and each estate—for estate tax purposes—is entitled to use their coupon. In other words, for a married couple each spouse has an applicable exclusion amount—the IRS grocery store coupon. Very similar to a lot of supermarkets and grocery stores, the IRS also has "double coupon days." It's a little bit like playing IRS Supermarket bingo. How much is your coupon worth, where is it, and when should you use it?

The Marital Deduction

Certain transfers from one spouse to the other spouse qualify for the marital deduction for both estate and gift tax purposes. Currently the marital deduction is an unlimited amount. The following things qualify for the marital deduction:

- Outright transfers between spouses.

- Insurance proceeds payable to a surviving spouse.

- Transfers between spouses by virtue of joint ownership.

- Spousal beneficiary designations on most retirement plan benefits.

- Transfers in trust for a spouse.

Makes you wish you were Bill and Melinda Gates, doesn't it?

For estate tax purposes and for marital deduction purposes, it is important to understand the distinction between two types of powers of appointment; a general power of appointment and a non-general power of appointment. Essentially a public power of appointment allows you to redirect assets and bequests that you would otherwise receive to someone else or to a trust for someone else's benefit. Michigan has legislation dealing with powers of appointment: the Powers of Appointment Act.

In the case of the marital deduction, if a husband dies and leaves a portion of his estate in a life estate with a general power of appointment trust for the benefit of his spouse, the assets that go into that trust will qualify for the marital deduction in the husband's estate when he dies. Subsequently when the spouse dies the assets remaining in that trust at that time will be included for estate tax purposes in the spouse's estate.

Again, remember that under United States versus Windsor and Obergefell versus Hodges, and also subsequent guidance issued by the IRS, same-sex couples legally married under the laws of their state may take advantage of all the same benefits previously enjoyed only by opposite-sex married couples.

As previously discussed, the ability of the surviving spouse to use the remaining amount of the IRS grocery store coupon of the deceased spouse is available if the election is made by the personal representative of the deceased spouse on a timely filed IRS 706 estate tax return. Interestingly, to claim the unused coupon amount, the personal representative of the pre-deceased spouse will need to file the estate tax return even if the predeceased spouse's estate is not taxable.

FWPP practitioners should address and integrate this portability planning in their plans. The FWPP documents for married couples should address the question of whether the personal representative should be required to elect this technique or at least be given the discretion to do so.

Tax Returns

A gift tax return must be filed if a gift to anyone, other than the spouse of the gift giver, exceeds the current annual gift tax exclusion and does not qualify for the other exclusions for education or medical expenses. A gift tax return must be filed if there is a gift that is not even a gift of a present interest regardless of the value of the gift. The gift tax return is IRS form 709. It must be filed on or after January 1 and before April 15 of the year following the year of the gift. Copies of any and all gift tax returns should be saved until the taxpayer dies. This is because federal transfer taxes are cumulative, and all gift and estate tax returns require knowledge of any prior taxable transfers.

A federal gift tax return must be filed even if there is no tax due if the gross estate of the deceased person exceeds the coupon amount. That return is IRS form 706. And remember, as previously noted, the decision to give the unused portion of your coupon to your spouse is made by filing a timely federal estate tax return. This form, and any taxes, are due nine months from the date of death. You can obtain an automatic extension of six months by filing IRS form 4768.

Other Taxes

Federal Income Tax

The type of revocable living trust that we have discussed in this book is not a separate income tax payer while it is still revocable and amendable. When the trust is established by the trustmaker, he or she reserves the right to amend and revoke the trust. Because of these reserved powers, the IRS uses the term "grantor trust" for federal income tax purposes, which means the trustmaker is treated as the owner of the trust. All of the income, deductions, and credits of the trust are attributable to the trustmaker and are picked up on his or her personal income tax return. Usually, when assets are titled in the name of the trust, the trustmaker's Social Security number is used.

In most cases, the trustee of a revocable living trust does not file a separate income tax return. However, if a bank is the sole trustee, it will normally get a separate tax payer identification number, file a separate income tax return for the trust, IRS form 1041, and report the items of income, deductions, and credits that are attributable to the trustmaker on a separate attachment to the Form 1041.

When there is only one trustmaker who is treated as the owner of the trust and if the trustmaker is the trustee or one of multiple trustees, a Form 1041 is not filed. Instead, the trustmaker simply reports the income, deductions, and credits on his or her tax return just as he or she did before the trust was established. When a person dies, the income he or she received up to and including the date of death, including income from a trust the decedent is treated as having owned, is reported on the decedent's final income tax return, which covers the period from January 1 of the year of the date of death. Income received after the date of death from assets that were jointly owned by the decedent and another is reported on the other owner's joint tax return. In the case of a married couple, the surviving spouse is able to file a joint return for the year of the other spouse's death. That return includes the decedent's income up to the date of death and the surviving spouse's income for the entire year.

Income that is received by the decedent's estate and by his or her trust is taxed to the estate and the trust. When the trustmaker dies, that person's trust becomes irrevocable, and it becomes a new taxpayer subject to the separate rules that govern the income taxation of trusts and estates.

Normally Probate estates and trusts that are separate taxpayers must obtain a new taxpayer identification number. And, if required, file the tax returns discussed previously on Form 1041. An estate or trust reports income very similar to the way an individual reports income. In other words, the same types of income are reported on Form 1041. Some deductions are also available.

Michigan Property Taxes

Michigan property taxes come into play in the FWPP context because of the principal residence exemption on the taxable value of the principal residence. Michigan law provides an exemption from local school operating taxes for a principal residence. A separate section of the law provides an exemption for qualified agricultural property. Agricultural property is unoccupied property classified as agricultural or unoccupied property that is devoted primarily—as in more than fifty percent of the acreage—to agricultural use. A homeowner can also claim an additional exemption for up to three years on property previously exempt as their principal residence if the property is unoccupied and remains for sale.

A home that is owned by the occupant's revocable living trust still qualifies for the principal residence exemption. The affidavit which is filed for the principal residence exemption should list the trustmaker as the owner and his or her Social Security number. A life beneficiary is also considered the owner and is entitled to claim the exemption. A very useful tool for answering questions about the principal residence exemption can be found in the Michigan Department of Treasury's Guidelines for the Michigan Principal Residence Exemption Program.

16

NO FAMILY WEALTH PROTECTION PLAN?

The State of Michigan Has One For You

Hope is not a strategy.

Rudy Giuliani, Mayor of New York

Many people die without having a FWPP. They die without even leaving a simple will or without addressing a more complete will substitute plan as we discussed in this book. Many people simply do not take the time to even begin to plan, always saying "I'll get around to it." A picture of a round "TUIT" can be found at the end of this chapter, with a simple explanation of how we view that statement. We have also heard that many people would like to plan but simply do not know how to go about it, or whom to ask. Many people simply do not get around TUIT. The same is certainly true of planning for disability. People do not plan for disability for the same reasons they don't plan for death: they simply just don't take the time to address it, learn about it, or get around TUIT.

If you do not plan your own estate, for either your death or your disability, the Michigan legislature has planned it for you. As we meet many of these hardened non-planners as part of our practice, we are often tempted to say: Worry not, plan not, don't worry, be happy—if that is your choice—because the State of Michigan already has a plan made to dispose of your property for you via Michigan law, called the Estate and Protected Individuals Code (EPIC), which describes in great detail what happens to your property if there is no simple will or other type of will or will substitute. We believe that the statement, "failure to plan is planning to fail" is not a cliché. The State of Michigan's plan is generally referred to as a statute of intestacy, i.e. the "no plan/ plan." As a result, EPIC will distribute the property of non-planners to the State of Michigan delineated heirs. The result can, and normally is, quite discomforting.

In order to illustrate how this works, let's examine EPIC and apply it to the following family situation:

The soon-to-be deceased person and his spouse are in their middle 40s. They have one teenager and two small children. A paternal grandmother is also part of the family. She has lived happily in their home for seven years and derives her support mainly from the soon-to-be deceased person.

Now, of course the unexpected happens. The deceased-to-be becomes deceased. The tragedy has in fact occurred, and there is of course no will, no plan, no nothing. Wait; yes, there is. It is the State of Michigan's plan reproduced here with a little bit of fun, artistic license, and only a touch of exaggeration.

Last Will of Roger Round Tuit

First: I direct the Probate Judge to appoint anyone of his choosing to administer all property in my name and distribute it under the terms of this will.

Second: I direct that all of my assets be converted to cash, all of my debts paid, including taxes, probate fees, administrative fees, and attorney's fees, out of this cash.

Third: My surviving spouse or partner <u>may</u> be named personal representative of my estate or may not be. If they are named, they will be responsible for administering and managing the estate during the probate process. All of their actions will be subject to the scrutiny and approval of the court, its officials, and other government employees.

Fourth: My surviving spouse or partner will perhaps be named the guardian of the children by the court. If named, they will be allowed to manage the children's property as their conservator for their benefit, also, of course, under the scrutiny of the court, its officials, and government employees.

Fifth: I direct that one-half, if I am survived by one child, or one-third, if I am survived by two or more children, of my property, be paid to my spouse or partner.

Sixth: I direct that the balance of my estate be distributed outright, and in cash, in equal shares to my children. If any child is a minor, I direct that their share be held by a guardian for their benefit. The guardian may be anyone of the Probate Judge's choosing.

Seventh: When each of my minor children attains age eighteen, I direct that their share be paid to them outright, regardless of their financial circumstances or emotional maturity.

Eighth: In the event my spouse or partner does not survive me, I direct that their share be added to the children's shares under the other articles.

Ninth: I direct that my surviving spouse or partner will be required to render periodic accountings to the probate court about most of their actions. The court shall have the right to ask questions about what they have done, and the court's determination with regard to those answers will be final.

Tenth: If none of my children survive me but my spouse or partner does, I direct that the remainder of my estate be distributed outright in the following manner:

A. One-half of my property to my spouse or partner;

B. The balance to my parents, if living, otherwise to my brothers, sisters, or their heirs.

Eleventh: If I am not survived by my spouse or partner, children or parents, I direct the Probate Court to seek out any and all of my closest blood relatives and divide my estate among them in a way that gives them the share according to the laws of the State of Michigan and their descendants.

Twelfth: If no relatives are located, I direct that all of my property go to the State of Michigan.

Thirteenth: Should my spouse or partner remarry, the new spouse or partner may be entitled to all funds previously given by the spouse to the deceased spouse or partner. Should my spouse or partner also rely on Michigan's will upon their death, the local probate court shall decide who will raise the children.

Fourteenth: All property shall be subject to the control and resulting costs and fees of the probate court. All court costs, attorney's fees, accounting fees, accountants' fees, and other expenses shall be paid out of the children's funds.

Signed, Your all-seeing, all-knowing Michigan legislature.

Please keep in mind that the obviously ridiculous results of the Michigan legislature can be avoided with a little planning, if only we could convince the hardened non-planners to merely take a few hours to plan. Another problem with the Michigan legislature will is determining which state's law is going to control the assets of the deceased non-planner. Each of the states has the right to control the real property located within its borders. Land and buildings are, of course, real property. If our hardened non-planner owns a cabin in another state, that other state's law and courts will control the disposition of the cabin. States are of course protective and jealous as to the property and soil within their borders, as well as their laws, taxation, and other matters that apply to that soil.

Another problem our hardened non-planner faces is determining which state's law will control their personal property. The state in which the non-planner lived determines where the personal property will pass. Where did the non-planner really live? As attorneys we would ask where was the person's domicile? Domicile is the chief number one, absolute, true residence of a citizen. There can be only one domicile, and it is sometimes hard to establish. States can fight over which laws apply if no domicile is clear. The state that wins of course collects the taxes and the death taxes and the other fees and circumstances regarding that personal property.

If you become disabled, meaning you cannot take care of yourself or your financial affairs because of mental or other problems, the state also has a remedy for you. You see, when you are disabled, you cannot make personal decisions about your own health or physical well-being. Additionally, you cannot manage your own financial affairs; it's likely, for example, you cannot even sign checks or buy and sell your own assets. Someone must be made legally responsible for you and must do that for you.

As we discussed in Chapter 6, that person typically will be appointed by the local probate court. You will need both a personal guardian and a financial guardian. The probate court will then supervise your care and your finances under its rules rather than according to your desires. Of course, the people or institutions that the court appoints will be assumed to be looking out for your best interest. However, as you might expect, the system is cumbersome, crowded, and not necessarily designed for compassion and support. Similar to dying without a will or any other planning, experiencing an unplanned disability can result in a great deal of sadness, misunderstanding, expense, and turmoil.

The point of this chapter is that the Michigan legislature and the Michigan probate court system are always a poor substitute for your own planning and desires. Perhaps the Michigan legislature, in its zeal to assist the non-planning citizens, has given false security to too many people. Maybe the State of Michigan should say: "If you don't plan it, we will take it and put it in the general fund."

So again, at the expense of repeating ourselves, perhaps Roger Round TUIT should consider applying the six Ps: proper prior planning prevents poor performance.

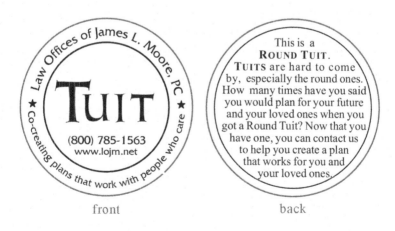

Law Offices of James L. Moore, PC

★ Co-creating plans that work with people who care ★

TUIT

(800) 785-1563
www.lojm.net

This is a ROUND TUIT. TUITS are hard to come by, especially the round ones. How many times have you said you would plan for your future and your loved ones when you got a Round Tuit? Now that you have one, you can contact us to help you create a plan that works for you and your loved ones.

front   back

17

WILLS

The lawsuit you file against yourself

If you always do what you've always done,
you'll always get what you've always got.

Henry Ford

enerally, a will is a set of written instructions created under certain legal formalities which directs how a person's property will be disposed of upon their death. "Last will and testament" is the common legal term for a will, based on an old phrase meaning essentially I dispose of my property.

Wills have to be very carefully written. Many people want to know if they can write their own wills. The answer is, absolutely! As long as you know exactly what you're doing and follow all of the formalities required by Michigan's laws. However, wills, being a special creation of the law, are fraught with technical difficulties, formal procedures, and other requirements which if not followed make the will invalid. Consequently, do-it-yourselfers should leave the drafting to professionals. Very few of the self-drawn or online forms of wills we have actually seen work at all, nor do they accomplish what the will maker intended. We like to say that Google is not a lawyer. Secondly, any type of online or do-it-yourself program that produces legal documents, especially a will, doesn't care whether your plan will actually work. Nor can it actually counsel you about what the document should say in the first place.

Historically, and interestingly, for many many years most people were unable to leave their property to their loved ones at all. On their death, much of their property passed to royalty. In 1540, the English Parliament passed legislation called the Statute of Wills; essentially, this statute allowed people the right, under a strict body of rules, to in fact pass their property to other people upon their death.

At the time this legislation was revolutionary. The rules adopted were complex. And of course, the lawsuits that followed as society began getting comfortable with this concept made the law even larger and more complex. Does this sound familiar in terms of today's government—its rules, regulations and unprecedented growth and interference with our daily lives?

A will only controls property that actually belonged to its maker, with one noteworthy exception. If someone else left property for you to use during your lifetime and specifically gave you the right to dispose of it upon your death, you have a power of appointment; that is, you have the right to say in your will who gets that property.

Wills do not control all property that goes to others by other planning devices or by operation of law. For example, jointly held property is not controlled by a will. Jointly held property automatically belongs to the other joint owners upon death. The same is true of property owned in a tenancy by the entireties, a special form of joint tenancy providing some creditor protection under the terms of Michigan law. Similarly, life insurance proceeds are not controlled by a will if the owner names a beneficiary other than their estate.

As we have stated, homemade do-it-yourself wills usually do not work or, at best, do not work very well. Joint wills can also create tremendous planning nightmares, especially in the area of taxation. But as previously discussed, what we call mythical wills or online forms or do-it-yourself forms can sometimes be hard to resist. We've all seen the advertisements on television or have seen them show up in our email inbox. Just send in your $50, fill in the blanks in the above form, forget about all of the two or three pages of disclaimer language at the bottom of this advertisement, sign it. Doesn't it feel terrific to get around all those scoundrel lawyers? Well, as we like to say in our office, "How's that going for you?"

Some people ask if they can merely amend an old will. The legal term for that is called a codicil. It is merely a desire of someone to alter their will without re-creating the entire document over again. However there is a big but; codicils must be drafted, signed, and prepared with all, and not less than all, the formalities of the original will.

The other concern we have with wills is that they are public documents. Typically, the contents of a will are not made public while the will maker is alive. However, on the death of the willmaker the will must be filed with the local probate court and its contents made part of the public record, which anyone and everyone can read if they want to. Thus your private business becomes the public's business. Not only is the will itself made public but all assets and debts as well as all of the proceedings disposing of them in the people to whom they are going are also made public.

We do not think that making everything about someone's family public is a very good idea. Anyone, with good intentions or bad, can thus know a family's intimate financial affairs. It doesn't seem to be a very sound practice to us, but you be the judge. Wills are also not effective until the will maker is actually deceased. Most people would like a little current benefit from their planning, especially in view of the energy and time and money required to plan in the first place. In our view wills provide little or no current benefits.

Additionally, wills simply cannot provide for the care of their makers. What if you get sick for a period of time or lose your ability to reason or conduct your affairs? Your will cannot help you. It only controls property you own after you die. While you are alive, it has no effect whatsoever.

A will that is valid in the state in which it was made is also valid in other states under current law. The only problem is determining whether the other state will follow their laws or the laws of the state under which the will was actually drafted. Unfortunately, the former is often the choice.

Assume that Roger Round TUIT has a will drafted in Michigan where he lives. Then assume that Roger and his family moved to Florida. Roger of course does not have his will redrafted, and then dies a resident of Florida. Consequently, Florida law, not Michigan law, may control the disposition of the estate. This result can be disastrous at times. We do not believe that wills are viable interstate planning tools. People move around. Americans are getting more mobile all the time. They seek opportunities on their own and of course are frequently relocated by their employers. Even deeply rooted, self-employed folks retire and are known to relocate to find that better climate.

There is a need for interstate flexibility in FWPP. Wills simply cannot provide this flexibility. However, a living trust does (see Chapter 4).

Wills must also go through the entire probate process. In meeting with clients and during seminars and workshops we have found that most people have the notion that to prepare a will is the way to avoid the probate court. This is definitely not true. The property that passes pursuant to the terms of your will must go through probate. We often say that the will is a compass that points at the courthouse.

Probate is a process of passing title from the will maker to others. The idea is that through the probate process, title to the will maker's property will be passed according to their wishes. Without a will the probate court will pass title the legislature's way, as previously discussed. Either way, with or without a will, your property has to go through the process of probate. Please believe us that the probate process can be a needlessly expensive and time-consuming process and that it can in fact be avoided.

Many attorneys recommend that clients leave their original wills with them. We do not believe this is a good practice. A law office is not safe from vandalism, theft, or a well-intended but fatal housekeeping process, or fire. A misplaced will amongst oftentimes hundreds of other files may just be misplaced. But it is lost until it's found. Your will is of critical importance to you and your family but only one among many in the attorney's office.

We could of course write an entire volume just on wills, but others have already done that. Besides, obviously, we are not at all keen on wills in the first place. They are all right, and they do work, and they have been around for hundreds of years, but there are several features that we believe are unattractive and unavoidable.

To summarize, wills:

- Are only effective on death.

- May not control all property.

- Involve complex legal rules.

- Are public.

- Do not work as interstate planning tools.

- Must go through probate.

- Can be subject to the claims of creditors and predators.

In our experience, many people, and most professional advisors who do not specialize in FWPP, still equate the estate planning process merely with the drafting of the last will and testament. They somehow believe that estate planning is will planning, even though that is an outdated view of the entire process.

It has been our experience in countless situations either one-on-one or during seminars and workshops when we have asked the question, "Do you have an existing estate plan?" The response has been, "Yes, I have a will, but it's out of date," or, "No, I've never had a will in the first place." The belief that FWPP and will drafting are synonymous is unfortunate and in most instances completely incorrect.

A will is but one method of disposing of property upon your death. In our experience, most people generally give little or no thought at all to other methods as they relate to the FWPP.

18

GIVING IT TO CHARITY

Pay It Forward

*Man does not simply exist but always decides
what his existence will be.*

Victor Frankl, Holocaust survivor

In a society attuned to charity, it is only logical that there is a tremendous variety of methods available to all of us to make charitable giving attractive. This chapter is aimed at the person who wants to obtain a 20,000-foot view of the vast income tax, gift tax, and estate tax opportunities available by making gifts to charity.

Charitable giving falls into some general categories, which include outright gifts, and gifts of a part of an interest in property. All these may be used during one's lifetime or at one's death. Each has its own separate federal income tax, gift tax, and estate tax implications. Outright gifts of property are probably the most commonly used form of giving, and people making an outright gift can make their gifts in money or personal or real property.

To receive all of the tax benefits that can result from a charitable gift, the gift must be made to an Internal Revenue Code qualified charity. That is, the charity must be a public, semi-public, or private foundation that has received special approval from the IRS. A lifetime charitable gift has two distinct tax advantages. The first is that an income tax deduction is generated. The second is that those assets, along with their future appreciation, are removed from the value of your estate.

Normally, the income tax deduction that can be taken by the giver is limited to fifty percent of adjusted gross income (AGI).

There's another income tax deduction limitation that can apply when giving property to charity. It applies generally to property which, if sold, would be taxed at the capital gains rate.

When giving unappreciated property or property subject to capital gains, real estate, or any other type of property, part of the deduction advantage that you can obtain depends on current IRS guidelines. Certain limits and percentages apply depending on the type of the gift, and the exact nature of the charity to which the gift is being given. That's why it's important to have a qualified income tax professional assist you in this area together with your FWPP attorney.

There are further limitations on the amount that you can deduct when making a gift of appreciated property to a public charity. One example is that, if you give a work of art to a hospital, your deduction is limited. This is because the hospital cannot generally use artwork to further its exempt purposes. You can only deduct the original cost of the work of art.

As you might expect, these income tax rules are not exhaustive. A lot of other income tax rules can come into play, depending on the nature of the property and the type of charity to which you are giving it. For example, giving away real property and some other types of personal property which you have owned for less than one year can possibly trigger another tax called the alternative minimum tax, which may result in making the gift less attractive from a tax perspective. Again, you can see how important is for you to consult a tax advisor before making a charitable gift or other gift of cash.

Charitable giving almost always has some income tax ramifications. Direct charitable giving, providing it follows the rules, never results in any gift taxes. An outright gift upon death has no income tax advantages or disadvantages. But for federal estate tax purposes the value of the gift made to a qualified charity does result in a deduction equal to the fair market value of the gift.

If the charitably minded individual is in ill health and may not live, a lifetime charitable gift should be considered instead of a charitable gift at death. A lifetime gift has the potential advantage of reducing income taxes as well as reducing the giver's estate for federal estate tax purposes.

Many people want to give property to a charity at their deaths but want to retain the property for their use during their lifetimes. They would also like, if possible, to receive a current income tax deduction. The Internal Revenue Code allows for both of these benefits through the gift of a remainder interest to charity. A gift of a remainder interest that is not held in a trust is restricted to a former personal residence. This type of gift allows the giver to retain a life estate in the property. Consequently, the giver can use the property, receive income from the property, and live on the property during their lifetime. At the death of the giver, the property automatically passes to the charity.

How does the IRS go about calculating some of these deductions for this remainder interest? The value of the remainder interest can be determined under Internal Revenue Code guidelines. General evaluation is based on the life expectancy of the person who gives away the property. If a husband and wife or partners are joint givers, their joint life expectancy can also be calculated. The value of the remainder interest is the deductible expense used in the year the interest is given away. In addition to this income tax advantage, the asset passes to charity at death and is consequently removed from the estate of the giver.

Gifts to charity from a trust can take many forms. In our experience, the most commonly used charitable trusts are the remainder trust and the lead trust. The rules that govern these techniques and trusts are of course extremely complex, so the following brief discussion is directed only toward a basic understanding of their principles.

Charitable Remainder Trust

A Charitable Remainder Trust is a trust to which the trustmaker transfers income-producing property and then retains an income interest in the trust's property for the trustmaker or the trustmaker's family. The income interest retained by the giver or the giver's family is a fixed amount of the value of the property at the time it is transferred to the trust. The trust is called a charitable remainder annuity trust.

When the income interest that is retained by the giver or the giver's family can vary depending on changes in the annual value of the trust fund, the trust is called a charitable remainder unitrust. Regardless of which trust is used, the income must be at least five percent of the value of the property in the trust.

A charitable remainder annuity trust is less useful during inflationary times because of its inflexibility. It tends to benefit the charity more than the giver or the giver's family because inflation increases the value of the trust, but the income distributions are fixed as a percentage of the value of the trust property when the property was originally placed in the trust. Consequently, more of the trust property is ultimately left to charity.

A charitable remainder unitrust, however, tends to favor the giver and the giver's family because the income distributions increase as the trust assets increase. In both these types of remainder trusts, the beneficiaries of the trusts have a life-time interest in a percentage value of the assets. At death, the remaining trust assets pass automatically to the named charity.

All charitable remainder trusts are similar to remainder interests in property. The income belongs to the beneficiaries, and whatever is left belongs to charity. There is an income tax deduction available to the giver at the time the property is put into the trust in the amount of the present value of the remainder interest. As discussed earlier, this amount can be calculated using Internal Revenue Code guidelines.

Charitable Lead Trust

A charitable lead trust is the reverse of a charitable remainder trust. Instead of providing income to the beneficiaries and giving the property to charity, a lead trust gives income to the charity for a period of time and passes the property to the giver's beneficiaries, free of federal estate tax.

A lead trust involves valuing the remainder interest of the property to be placed in the trust. As previously mentioned, it is possible to value the remainder interest of such property. The value of the remainder interest in this case, however, results in a taxable gift to the beneficiaries. Is a gift of a future interest and therefore is not eligible for the annual gift tax exclusion. If the lead trust is structured properly with thorough counseling by a professional planner, however, the gift tax, in many instances, can be virtually eliminated.

The value of the income tax interest in a charitable lead trust must also be valued. The value of the income interest may be income tax deductible to the giver in the year the property is placed in the trust. The big limitation is, however, that the giver only gets an income tax deduction in the year the property was given to the trust. After that, in future years, the income is taxed to the giver. Because of this income tax disadvantage, many people elect not to take the income tax deduction. If that is their decision, and the trust is drafted correctly, none of the lead trust income will be taxed to them.

This trust can be beneficial for several reasons: the maker removes property from their estate, free of federal estate tax, while passing it to chosen beneficiaries. And the charity has full use of all the income from the property. Charitable giving is a growing and broad area, encompassing not only federal estate and gift tax planning but also federal income tax planning. The smorgasbord of charitable giving techniques is limited only by one's imagination and, as always, certain provisions of the Internal Revenue Code. And again, as always, if you are genuinely interested in discussing or examining the possibility of using charitable giving as part of your FWPP, be sure to seek expert assistance.

19

WEALTH RECEPTION[6]

Throwing the Football

The beginning is the most important part of the work.

Plato

In some cases you may want to use a technique that involves a discretionary trust to plan for your children. Discretionary trust is defined as an irrevocable trust in which someone other than the trustmaker is the trustee, and the trustee has complete discretion to make, or not make, distributions to one or more beneficiaries.

---

6 *Chapter 19 contains information provided by J. David Kerr, Esq., The Kerr Law Firm.*

Traditional Estate Planning

Transfer Assets

Disability

Retirement

Children's Needs

© 2006 J. David Keer

This requires you to look at passing on your estate from a different perspective by standing in the shoes of the person receiving the assets. Looking from the perspective of reception, what can we plan and do now to positively affect what value is received and how that value is received?

With proper planning you can create a "lock box" that is controlled by the trustee and then later have your revocable living trust "pour-over" into the wealth reception trust. The idea here is that it is never too late and there is always the opportunity to serve the beneficiary, enhance the reception of value by the beneficiary, and help them develop a relationship with your other advisors that should last a lifetime.

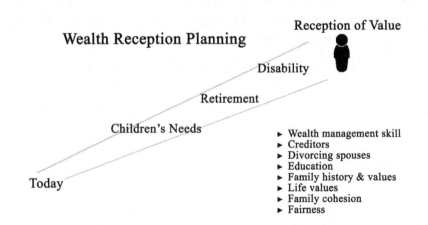

Wealth Reception Planning

Reception of Value

Disability

Retirement

Children's Needs

Today

- ► Wealth management skill
- ► Creditors
- ► Divorcing spouses
- ► Education
- ► Family history & values
- ► Life values
- ► Family cohesion
- ► Fairness

Uses of Discretionary Trusts

- Protect trust assets from creditors, predators, and outlaws while making benefits available to a beneficiary.

- Provide an education tool for beneficiaries who do not have extensive investment experience.

- Protect the government assistance for which a beneficiary may qualify while making assets or benefits available to that person.

- The trustee is the legal owner of the trust assets.

- The trustee may permit the beneficiary the use of the assets owned in the trust.

The use concept is valuable for asset protection, education, qualification for government assistance, and beneficiary spending protection.

An example of how this might work is to view and use the discretionary trust as an education tool for the beneficiaries by establishing the trust now and then using "Crummey Powers" similar to how we structure an ILIT (see Chapter 14), and then allow the beneficiaries, working with a financial planner, to invest the trust assets. The trustee has total discretion and may pay income or the total return from the trust to the beneficiaries. The trust may, or may not, include ILIT purchase of life insurance powers, which makes the whole structure an education tool for beneficiaries while you are still alive and well.

Regarding discretion, the trustee, or another designated person, determines both the amount and form of the distributions. There is Michigan law to support the idea that a pure third-party discretionary trust cannot be reached by creditors or predators.

To ensure that these advantages are realized the trustee must have active duties relating to administration and accounting, investment, and distribution. Obviously, if the trustee must make distribution decisions, the trustee has an active duty. The point is to ensure that there are several specific duties to make sure it cannot be interpreted to be merely a "passive trust."

Regarding special needs beneficiaries, because the trust is established by a third party, and third-party funds are used, no compliance is required with technical special needs statutory requirements. However, the special needs beneficiary cannot be the source of the funds going into the trust. Thus, it is best to not even use the term special needs in the trust document.

Regarding the situation where the beneficiary may have a history of poor money management or of being a spendthrift:

- A properly drafted discretionary trust can serve as a very strong lock box to protect the assets.

- The trustee can provide conditions for payment.

- Separate directions to the trustee may be useful.

Obviously, the selection of a trustee is critical and should include the following considerations:

- Wisdom to implement the trustmaker's intentions.

- Strength to withstand attempts to persuade while still focusing on proper objectives.

- Separate directions to the trustee may be useful.

It's best to have not only lifetime discussions with the trustee regarding your goals and desires for the beneficiary, but also to provide a letter of instruction to the trustee. It may even be best to provide separate letters relating to each beneficiary. Additional protection can be provided by adding trust protector provisions to the trust agreement itself.

It's also important to provide for flexibility over time. We talk about three universal rules: People are different, things change, and everyone dies. The "things" that change normally involve the beneficiaries and their circumstances, financial investments and products, and improvements in professional experience and thinking. That being said, we recommend that the trust be properly drafted so that even though irrevocable it can be changed. However, the trustmaker should not and usually cannot make such changes. The trust can provide for changes by the trust protector, trust advisor, or trust committee. Lastly, despite these benefits and advantages, discretionary trusts are not common. For example, most bank trust departments dislike discretionary trusts because they want to use their own standards to avoid any potential liability.

If this topic is of interest to you, we encourage you to take the time to get with your FWPP expert and unpack it further.

20

GIVING PROPERTY
TO MINORS

Tough Love—Tough Choices

*The little reed, bending to the force of the wind,
soon stood upright again when the storm passed over.*

Aesop

If it were even possible to do so, an experienced FWPP professional would perhaps make a generalized statement that in their experience most people want their property to ultimately end up in the hands of their children and grandchildren. Almost every simple will we have reviewed over the years was basically an I love you will—as in I leave all my property to my spouse or partner but if they do not survive me I leave it equally to my children. And if any child of mine dies leaving children, I want their share to go to his or her children—my grandchildren.

Almost every life insurance contract we have reviewed has named beneficiaries in the same manner. The purpose of this chapter is to discuss the problems associated with gifting or leaving property directly to minor children or grandchildren. Under the current system of law, giving your property to minor beneficiaries is not easy.

Michigan law defines minors as persons who have not yet attained the age of 18. Can you make an outright gift of property to your minor children or grandchildren? The answer is both yes and no. Yes, in that you can do anything you want to with your property. No, unless you follow the legal formalities under current Michigan law for making such a gift. Under Michigan law, in order to make a gift of more than a nominal amount to a minor, you must take one of five steps.

Set Up a Uniform Gift to Minors Account

This custodial account has generally been used to make gifts of stock, but in Michigan can also be used to hold cash, securities, and some types of annuity contracts. An adult custodian must be named on the account with the minor. The custodian manages the account until the minor becomes an adult. A new version of the Uniform Gifts to Minors Act has been enacted in Michigan. Under this newer version of the law, nearly all types of property, including real estate, can be titled in the name of the custodian on behalf of the minor.

Create a Savings Account Trust

The savings and loan association law provides liberalized handling of accounts created in the name of a minor. These accounts can be established in the name of the minor, and the minor is entitled to make deposits or withdrawals in the same manner as an adult without any liability to the savings and loan association.

Establish a Totten Trust

An account called a Totten trust can be established with a commercial bank or savings and loan association. This type of account is created by registering the account in a particular form. For example, "John Jones, in Trust for Mary Jones." In Michigan, it is usually presumed that the account belongs to the adult person named as trustee, unless it can be shown that the trust was intended to be irrevocable. On the death of the adult trustee, the account proceeds belong to the minor but are controlled by the local probate court on behalf of the minor until they reach adulthood.

Fund a Living Trust for the Benefit of the Minor Beneficiary

A living trust that is used to give property to minors is called a 2503(c) trust. It is named after the Internal Revenue Code section that allows the income from the trust to be taxed to the minor beneficiaries. The lower tax brackets make the potential savings attractive in some cases. There is no income tax benefit at all for children under fourteen years of age.

Petition the Probate Court to Authorize a Conservatorship

The court will name an adult conservator who will manage the property under the court's direction and supervision until the minor becomes an adult.

These techniques represent the alternatives available to you when it is your desire to give property to your minor children and grandchildren. If this brief review of these living techniques appears to be complex, just imagine how difficult it is to get your property into the hands of these minors on your death.

For example, if your will leaves property directly to minors or if your insurance proceeds are to be paid directly to minors, we can assure you that your minor beneficiaries will not directly receive anything. Michigan law will require that those funds receive the supervision of a court-directed conservatorship. Thus the court will supervise all matters relating to these funds.

If you neglected to name a guardian for your minor children and your will, the probate court will select a guardian on its terms—not yours. If you have more than one child, the court could potentially name a separate guardian for each child. Each court-appointed guardian will be totally responsible for all of their actions to an already overburdened and extremely busy probate judge.

If you were conscientious and named your choice of guardian in your will, but nevertheless left property directly to minor children, the court will have to supervise the distribution of that property.

The probate judge will appoint a conservator to administer your children's property. The conservator who is selected may be an adult person or a licensed institutional trustee. The person the judge selects will be responsible to the judge on an ongoing basis for all their acts with respect to the children's property. The custodian may or may not be the same person who has been named as the children's guardian.

A court-imposed conservatorship that results from leaving property directly to minors on death has, in our opinion, the following drawbacks:

- All your property and all the conservator's actions with respect to it are made public.

- The court may require that a bond be posted for each year of the conservatorship and that it be paid for from the children's funds.

- The conservator will have to keep detailed records of their transactions and will have to show those records to the court. This both takes time and costs money.

- The conservator will be paid out of the children's funds as well.

- The conservator is usually required to use the services of an attorney, and working with the court and any attorney's fees will be paid out of the children's funds.

- The conservator whom the court appoints may not be experienced in the investment of funds or may not have the best interests of the children at heart.

Leaving property directly to minors on death involves a great deal of red tape. It depersonalizes the planning process and can create confusion and insecurity in your loved ones. It can also generate substantial expenses and unreasonable delays. In all of our experience in dealing with both parents and grandparents, we are convinced they have very definite feelings with respect to how they want their children and grandchildren raised and provided for economically after their deaths. And yet so many people leave most of what they have directly to their minor children and grandchildren in the belief that somehow miraculously this property will be used for the direct care of the children and grandchildren. This assumption is mistaken.

Any parent or grandparent who seeks to leave property to a minor beneficiary should always seek out the assistance of a professional FWPP to accomplish those wishes through the creation of a properly drafted trust. Through the use of such a trust, the following are accomplished:

Parents and grandparents can give what they have to minor beneficiaries in the way they want and when they want. They can also control the disposition of their estates and create unique planning solutions to accommodate unique family planning objectives.

They can select the children's guardians and the person or persons who will invest and control the purse strings with respect to their property.

They can avoid the active control intervention of the probate court and keep their affairs and those of their beneficiaries out of the public's eye.

All expenses that result through a conservatorship are avoided; the only expense is the trustee's fees.

21

PLANNING FOR CHILDREN

Love and Family Principles Can Survive Disability & Death

If passion drives you, let reason hold the reins.

Benjamin Franklin

In discussing estate planning with our clients who have minor children, we have learned that most parents have very strong and definite values and ideas regarding how their children should be raised and provided for. Most people express significant concern regarding not only who should raise their children but also how the children will and would be economically provided for if neither parent were alive. These fears and anxieties with respect to the reality that would follow a catastrophic death are of course well-founded.

The responsibility of a professional estate planner includes helping parents to plan for their children in the event of the parent's death. This planning of course involves far more than just economics. Planning for minor children involves creating an environment that will allow minor loved ones to experience not only the tender loving care that goes with it, but also the economic security that will and should provide more than the mere necessities of life as they eventually grow into adulthood. This requires a tremendous amount of thought and responsibility to properly plan for potential orphans.

In this chapter, we discuss the techniques you can use to provide a substitute lifestyle for your minor loved ones. It is important to understand that your wishes can become reality after your death if you take the time now to plan properly.

Selecting a Guardian

It is essential that you take the time to select and name the person or persons whom you wish to raise your children in the event that you can't do so. These persons are called guardians. Under Michigan law, guardians need to be named in a will. Thus, when using a revocable living trust-based plan, the guardians should be named in the pour-over will that accompanies it.

It's not unusual for our clients to become slightly exasperated when asked, "Who do you want to raise and take care of your children both economically and emotionally in the event of your death?" They find it difficult while attempting to respond to think of anyone who, as a replacement parent, would do anywhere nearly as good a job as they could. Several people are often usually discussed and considered; all may end up discarded because of one deficiency or another. Often this results in no decision at all. And the parents, in frustration, come to this conclusion: "We don't know anyone who could properly raise our children anywhere nearly as well as we could."

Our normal response is, "We certainly understand where you're coming from, but please, after giving it much thought and after discussing it together, at least you can give us 'the best of the worst.'" It is essential that you select your children's guardian, because regardless of its drawbacks, your choice will, in all likelihood, be far better than the choice of a probate judge you've never met before, who knows nothing about your family, nor your values or beliefs. The point is, if you do not name a guardian, the court will. Yes, the selection of a guardian is a difficult process, but it must be done. In going through the process, we suggest the following:

Provide for a succession of guardians in your will. There is no guarantee that any one guardian will be alive and well when needed or that your chosen guardian will agree to serve in the first place. Always spell out your first, second, and if important to you, third choice of guardians in your will.

Always discuss your choices with the potential guardians you would like to name before you name them. This will ensure, to some degree, that they will in fact be able to and willing to serve if named.

Share your FWPP with the guardians you have named so they will know and understand what they're getting into.

It's best to select your guardians on the basis of their beliefs, morality, values, and lifestyle, not on their ability to manage a financial portfolio. Management of the children's funds will not necessarily be the responsibility of the guardians. Others can be named to manage the children's property as trustees. If you so choose, however, the guardians and the trustees can be the same persons.

If you elect to name a married couple as guardians, use both their full names and describe them in your will.

In Michigan, the guardians who are selected and named in the will do not serve automatically. The probate judge must, after an independent inquiry, approve and name the guardian. However, it is comforting to know that the parent's choice is presumptive and normally followed.

Leaving Property to Children

It is not a wise idea to ever leave property or insurance proceeds directly to your minor children. Always use a trust agreement to leave your property to minor loved ones. As discussed in the chapters on trusts, we believe that a revocable living trust should be used, for all the reasons we've already discussed.

By using a trust, you can spell out in great detail precisely how you wish your children to be taken care of and when you wish them to receive the balance of your property, if ever. You can also name both the individuals and/or institutions you would like to have manage the property for the benefit of your children. The trustees or financial guardians you name can and will work closely with the personal guardians and follow your instructions to provide for your children's well-being. What follows is a description of several of the techniques that are used in this area.

Dividing Property Among the Children

Many, if not most, of the wills and trusts we have reviewed on behalf of our clients divide the property up into equal but separate shares for each child immediately upon the death of the trustmaker. This technique reflects the trustmaker's intent to treat the children equally, and as a result, each child has a separate trust share that can only be used for that child's benefit. We believe that automatically adopting this type of planning sometimes is ill-conceived and does not accomplish what the parents had in mind if they were actually questioned and counseled about it. For example, what happens if one or more of the children has extraordinary needs for funds because of sickness or other unforeseen emergencies? The answer is that, under the normal technique, once their individual trust is depleted, they will become wards of the state. This would be true even though their brothers or sisters still have significant sums remaining in their trusts that they do not even need.

A better technique, in our opinion, is to leave all of your property in a common trust for the benefit of all your children, for their health, support, maintenance, education, and general welfare. In our office we call this trust a "Chicken Soup Pot" trust. Then later, once all of your children become adults, whatever is left can be divided equally among them and either given to them or placed in a separate trust for each of them to be distributed in accordance with your wishes.

The statement that "There is nothing so unequal as the equal treatment of unequals" certainly applies here. Normally, most parents, while they are alive and well, care for their children based on those individual children's needs rather than on the basis of an equal share or ledger book mentality. The resources of the parents are used to care for all the children based on those individual needs, not on a dollar-for-dollar accounting method. We believe that after death, this normal pattern should be no different.

After that, the timing of exactly when the chicken soup pot trust for the children should be divided into individual shares is a matter of individual preference based on counseling. For example, many of our clients believe that it should be divided when the youngest child reaches a certain age, twenty-three or twenty-five, for example. One technique that we have found to be particularly useful divides the common trust into separate shares when the youngest child either attains the age of twenty-three, or in the alternative, upon graduation from college, whichever occurs first. When you choose to divide the common trust is your decision. Important consideration in your FWPP is to make sure that all your children are provided for during the time they are minors and that they are provided for from all of your resources.

One of the questions that considering this technique frequently raises is, "Do my other children have to wait until their youngest brother or sister reaches that magic age before any of my adult children can get some of their money to invest in a business or to use for any other good purpose?" The answer is no, if the trust document is carefully written. Instructions can be given to the trustee to advance money to any of the other older children for the purposes that are enumerated in the trust instructions. In advancing the money, the trustee should be instructed to first be sure that enough common trust funds will be left to feed, clothe, educate, and care for minor brothers and sisters. A provision can also be included in the trust document to provide that upon the ultimate division of the common trust into separate shares for each of the children, any amounts advanced to adult children can reduce the amount of the shares that those adult children receive.

The choices available to you in this area are limited only by your imagination. The goal is to spur your thinking, ask you to become engaged in the counseling in this area, until you believe your purposes have been accomplished.

PART V

FAMILY WEALTH PROTECTION PLANNING SUMMARY

22

THE THREE STEP STRATEGY™ AND WHAT DO YOGI BERRA AND TEDDY ROOSEVELT HAVE TO SAY?

You have to be very careful if you don't know where you're going, because you might not get there.

Yogi Berra

W
e do not know of nor can we conceive of any generalized or average representative estate planning situation that can be used as an example or illustration to summarize all of the FWPP principles and techniques we have discussed. In our experience, most people have individual facts and circumstances and estates which of course then require individual counseling, design, and planning techniques.

However, there are certain basic universals common to the FWPP process. These can be summarized as follows:

- Inventory all of the assets that you own no matter how you own them.

- Know where all of the papers indicating the title to your assets are located, and understand how those assets have actually been titled.

- Michigan law provides an estate plan for you if you have not taken the time to plan to provide your own.

- If you choose to accomplish your planning by using a will, you should remember that wills are only effective on death and require the process previously described with all of its pitfalls. In addition, your will may not control all of your property.

- Also your will does not help you at all if you become disabled and are no longer able to handle your affairs. Absent additional customized disability planning you may have to face the inherent problems of a guardianship hearing at the probate court, which we have identified as living probate.

- Federal estate taxes are imposed on your right to transfer all of your property on death. The death tax is levied on the full fair market value of all your property and is generally paid within nine months of the date of death in cash; and it is of course paid before your beneficiaries receive anything.

- By using the IRS grocery store coupon, the death tax rules generally only apply to estates greater than $5 million, beginning January 1, 2013. The maximum tax bracket is forty percent. Spouses and domestic partners in all states can leave an unlimited amount of property to their U.S. citizen spouses or domestic partners tax-free, using a separate exemption in the Internal Revenue Code.

- The Federal estate and gift tax system has been unified since January 1, 2013. Thus, the IRS grocery store coupon and the IRS double coupon days deductions apply to gifts made during life as well as dispositions made on death.

- The law allows you also to make annual exclusion gifts to anyone of up to $14,000 without the requirement of filing a federal gift tax return. If your spouse or domestic partner chooses to split the gift with you, this amount doubles.

- All interest you have in any of your property will receive a step-up in its tax basis at your death.

- Trusts are truly the estate planner's toolbox because they can accomplish just about any of your objectives. Any number of separate trusts can be created in a single trust document. A living trust is created during your lifetime. A living trust that allows you the right to change your mind and thus change the trust is called a revocable living trust; one that cannot be changed is called an irrevocable living trust.

- A revocable living trust can provide for the control, coordination, and distribution of your property while you are alive and well, as well as on your death. It can also provide for your care and needs as well as those of your beneficiaries. Revocable living trusts are not public and are good in all states. They are extremely difficult for disgruntled heirs to attack.

- Your revocable living trust can be unfunded, partially funded, or totally funded during your lifetime. It can also be funded subsequent to your death. A fully funded revocable living trust avoids the probate process.

- Your trust planning will be only as good as the performance of your trustees. Trustees are totally responsible for fiduciary standards in expert performance and judgments while at the same time being required to follow the written babysitter instructions provided in your trust document. As superheroes, trustees have awesome power, accountability, and liability all wrapped together in this role.

- Both individual, personal, and institutional trustees have their strengths and weaknesses. You should select the types of trustees that best serve your planning purposes.

- Giving property to a minor can be difficult. Property left directly to a minor will be ambushed in a court-imposed custodianship until the minor reaches legal age. Involving a minor in the court process in any way shape or form creates and involves a great deal of red tape; depersonalizes the planning process; and normally creates confusion and insecurity for your loved ones while at the same time generating substantial expense and delay.

- When planning for children, you should provide for a succession of guardians and discuss your situation with the guardians that you choose; it's always a good idea to share all of your planning objectives with them.

- How you decide to divide and also distribute your property among your loved ones is of course your business. However, there are some general rules of thumb to follow: Do not divide your property among your children until the youngest is an adult. Once the property is divided, you can provide for different forms of distribution for each child to allow for specific thoughts and circumstances you may have with regard to each child. It's very important that you recognize that you can and should control how you wish your property to pass to your children and even your grandchildren.

- When planning for your spouse or domestic partner you should consider Michigan law and the rights it gives them to your property regardless of your planning attempts to the contrary. You may avail yourself of two planning techniques in this regard: prenuptial or postnuptial agreements.

- The number of planning possibilities available when planning for a spouse or partner is staggering. This is good news because it means there is no hypothetical best or optimal planning approach that can be used when planning for a spouse or partner today. Great care and extensive counseling should be taken and used to analyze all of the different possibilities available to you before you can select the best possible choice.

- Your life insurance program should be coordinated with and become a part of your total FWPP. Life insurance that you want on your own life will be included in your federal estate upon your death. It is important that you properly designate both primary and contingent beneficiaries.

- Life insurance can be purchased and structured to totally avoid federal estate tax. This is generally accomplished by the use of an irrevocable life insurance trust (ILIT). ILITs should be structured by estate planning specialists and can accommodate almost any type of insurance you may own.

- Unusual techniques are often not appropriate and do not work. These include cross-ownership of life insurance policies and joint tenancy, uniform gifts to minors act accounts, and general powers of attorney. There are also lots of estate planning tricks and gimmicks and other things that never seem to work at all. These include internet forms, cookie-cutter internet documents, bare-bones planning from general practice attorneys, hiding property in a safety deposit box, etc.

- Protecting your assets from creditors and predators is always and should always be a FWPP consideration. There are a number of ways that you can in fact protect your assets, including insurance, investing in exempt assets, and creating entities such as limited liability companies.

- Often, retirement plan benefits represent the largest asset in any estate. Knowledge about how to treat retirement plan benefits at the start of your FWPP is critical in creating an effective plan.

- If you desire to make contributions of cash or assets other than cash to qualified charities, either currently or on your death, you may receive some tax benefits. The rules surrounding the income tax, estate tax and gift tax deductibility of your desire to be charitable are extremely complex.

- FWPP is no place for lone rangers. Professional advisors should be selected for the knowledge and experience they possess within their disciplines. All of your advisors should participate in your FWPP process and should work well not only with you, but each other. The best knowledge tool we have found is a three-legged milking stool.

It may also be worthwhile for you to seek the advice and counsel of a collaborative group of professionals, such as the National Network of Estate Planning Attorneys, which is responsible for developing the Three Step Strategy outlined below, and who work together on a regular basis. These professionals should be from the law, accounting, insurance, and financial planning professions. This type of collaborative group will be able to help you far more than the traditional team of unrelated advisors.

THE FAMILY WEALTH PROTECTION PLANNING SOLUTION

THE THREE STEP STRATEGY™

It's Not About Documents - It's About Results

The key to creating a plan that works is clear, comprehensive, customized instructions for your own care and that of your loved ones. These instructions can be included in a will, a trust, and in several other related ancillary documents. We find that most of our clients are best served with a combination of these tools developed via the Three Step Strategy. "It's all about peace of mind, not a piece of paper."

STEP 1: DEVELOP

Develop your plan with counselling-oriented planning partners.

We believe much of what passes for estate planning in this country today is little more than word processing! We don't believe you should pay a licensed professional to do mere word processing. Their value is in their counsel and advice, based on knowledge, wisdom, and experience. If word processing is all you want, you may as well just do it yourself! But if you want a plan that works, seek good counseling from an attorney who is willing to work closely with other professionals such as your financial advisor and your accountant.

STEP 2. COMMIT

Commit yourself and your family to a formal, continuing maintenance and education program.

An estate plan faces a myriad of challenges. First, there is constant change in your personal, family, and financial situation. Second, there is constant change in both tax law and non-tax law that may impact your estate plan. Third, there is constant change in your attorney's experience and expertise. Your professional advisors are continually improving through ongoing education and their collective experience. Because everything constantly changes, you cannot expect a plan to accomplish what it was intended to accomplish if it is never updated. In fact, the costs of failing to update are typically far greater than the cost of keeping your plan current.

STEP 3: SECURE

Secure appropriate assistance to assure you and your family that your wisdom is transferred along with the rest of your wealth.

It's one thing to pass your financial wealth to the next generation. It's a different thing to pass it along in an orderly and protected manner. And it's yet another thing to pass along with it your wisdom, a critical part of your true wealth. A good estate plan accomplishes all three things.

By working with a team of professionals, your heirs will be able to receive their inheritance in a form that is protected from creditors and predators. In addition, you can structure your estate plan to provide in-depth instructions or commentary on those things that you believe are important for those heirs to know and do.

In any moment of decision the best thing you can do is the right thing. The next best thing you can do is the wrong thing. The worst thing you can do is nothing.

Teddy Roosevelt

Appendix A

Preparation for Planning Getting Organized

To print or download the following, please visit:

www.lawofficesofjamesmoore.com

Personal Information Form

Part I
Personal Information

Husband's Legal Name _____
(name most often used to title property and accounts)

Also Known As _____
(other names used to title property and accounts)

Prefer to be called _____ Birth date _____ SS# _____ US Citizen? _____

Home Address _____ City _____ State _____ Zip _____

Home Telephone _____ County of Residence _____ Business Telephone _____

Employer _____ Position _____

Business Address _____ City _____ State _____ Zip _____

E-mail Address _____ ❏ It is okay to communicate with me via my E-mail address.

Date of Marriage _____

Wife's Legal Name _____
(name most often used to title property and accounts)

Also Known As _____
(other names used to title property and accounts)

Prefer to be called _____ Birth date _____ SS# _____ US Citizen? _____

Home Address _____ City _____ State _____ Zip _____

Home Telephone _____ County of Residence _____ Business Telephone _____

Employer _____ Position _____

Business Address _____ City _____ State _____ Zip _____

E-mail Address _____ ❏ It is okay to communicate with me via my E-mail address.

Children and Other Family Members

(Use full legal name. Use "JT" if both spouses are the parents, "H" if husband is the parent, "W" if wife is the parent, "S" if a single parent.)

Name	Birth date	Parent or Relationship
_____	_____	_____
Comments: _____		
_____	_____	_____
Comments: _____		
_____	_____	_____
Comments: _____		
_____	_____	_____
Comments: _____		
_____	_____	_____
Comments: _____		

Advisors

	Name	Telephone
Personal Attorney	_____	_____
Accountant	_____	_____
Financial Advisor	_____	_____
Life Insurance Agent	_____	_____

Your Concerns

Please rate the following as to how important they are to you:
(H high concern, S some concerned, L low concern, N/A no concern or not applicable)

Description	Level of Concern	
	Husband	**Wife**
Desire to get affairs in order and create a comprehensive plan to manage affairs in case of death or disability.		
Providing for and protecting a spouse.		
Providing for and protecting children.		
Providing for and protecting grandchildren.		
Disinheriting a family member.		
Providing for charities at the time of death.		
Plan for the transfer and survival of a family business.		
Avoiding or reducing your estate taxes.		
Avoiding probate.		
Reduce administration costs at time of your death.		
Avoiding a conservatorship ("living probate") in case of a disability.		
Avoiding will contests or other disputes upon death.		
Protecting assets from lawsuits or creditors.		
Preserving the privacy of affairs in case of disability or at time of death from business competitors, predators, dishonest persons and curiosity seekers.		
Plan for a child with disabilities or special needs, such as medical or learning disabilities.		
Protecting children's inheritance from the possibility of failed marriages.		
Protect children's inheritance in the event of a surviving spouse's remarriage.		
Provide that your death shall not be unnecessarily prolonged by artificial means or measures.		

Other Concerns (Please list below):

_____

_____

_____

Law Office of James L. Moore, P.C.
3226 28th Street, SE, Kentwood, Michigan 49512
Phone: (800) 785-1563 ◆ Fax: (800) 785-1563

Important Family Questions

(Please check "Yes" or "No" for your answer)	Yes	No
Are you (or your spouse) receiving Social Security, disability, or other governmental benefits? *Describe* _____		
Are you (or your spouse) making payments pursuant to a divorce or property settlement order? *Please furnish a copy*		
If married, have you and your spouse signed a pre- or post-marriage contract? *Please furnish a copy*		
Have you (or your spouse) been widowed? *If a federal estate tax return or a state death tax return was filed, please furnish a copy*		
Have you (or your spouse) ever filed federal or state gift tax returns? *Please furnish copies of these returns*		
Have you (or your spouse) completed previous will, trust, or estate planning? *Please furnish copies of these documents*		
Do you support any charitable organizations now that you wish to make provisions for at the time of your death? *If so, please explain below.*		
Are there any other charitable organizations you wish to make provisions for at the time of your death? *If so, please explain below.*		
If married, have you lived in any of the following states while married to each other? *Arizona, California, Idaho, Louisiana, Nevada, New Mexico, Texas, Washington, or Wisconsin*		
Are you (or your spouse) currently the beneficiary of anyone else's trust? *If so, please explain below.*		
Do any of your children have special educational, medical, or physical needs?		
Do any of your children receive governmental support or benefits?		
Do you provide primary or other major financial support to adult children or others?		

Additional Information

_____
_____
_____
_____

Part II

Property Information

Instructions for completing the Property Information checklist:

General Headings

This **Property Information** checklist helps you list all the property you own and what it is worth. If you do not own property under a particular heading, just leave that section blank. Under certain headings, you may own more property than can be listed on this checklist. If so, attach extra sheets of paper to list your additional property.

Type

Immediately after the heading for each kind of property is a brief explanation of what property you should list under that heading.

"Owner" of Property

How you own your property is **extremely important** for purposes of properly designing and implementing your estate plan. For each property, please indicate how the property is titled. When doing so, please use the following abbreviations:

Owner of Property	Use
If married, Husband's name alone, with no other person	H
If married, Wife's name alone, with no other person	W
If married, Joint Tenancy with spouse	JTS
Joint Tenancy with someone other than a spouse, i.e. a child, parent, etc.	JTO
If you cannot determine how the property is owned	?

Real Property

TYPE: Any interest in real estate including your family residence, vacation home, timeshare, vacant land, etc.

General Description and/or Address	Owner	Market Value	Loan Balance
Total			

Furniture and Personal Effects

TYPE: List separately only major personal effects such as jewelry, collections, antiques, furs, and all other valuable non-business personal property *(indicate type below and **give a lump sum value for miscellaneous**, less valuable items.).*

Type or Description	Owner	Market Value
Miscellaneous Furniture and Household Effects (Total)		
Total		

Automobiles, Boats, and RVs

TYPE: For each motor vehicle, boat, RV, etc. please list the following: description, how titled, market value and encumbrance:

Bank Accounts

TYPE: Checking Account "CA", Savings Account "SA", Certificates of Deposit "CD", Money Market "MM" *(indicate type below). Do not include IRAs or 401(k)s here*

Name of Institution and account number	Type	Owner	Amount
		Total	

Note: If Account is in your name (or your spouse's name) for the benefit of a minor, please specify and give minor's name.

Stocks and Bonds

TYPE: List any and all stocks and bonds you own. If held in a brokerage account, lump them together under each account. *(indicate type below)*

Stocks, Bonds or Investment Accounts	Type	Acct. Number	Owner	Amount
			Total	

Life Insurance Policies and Annuities

TYPE: Term, whole life, split dollar, group life, annuity. **ADDITIONAL INFORMATION:** Insurance company, type, face amount (death benefit), whose life is insured, who owns the policy, the current beneficiaries, who pays the premium, and who is the life insurance agent.

Total _____

Retirement Plans

TYPE: Pension (P), Profit Sharing (PS), H.R. 10, IRA, SEP, 401(K). **ADDITIONAL INFORMATION:** Describe the type of plan the plan name, the current value of the plan, and any other pertinent information.

Total _____

Law Office of James L. Moore, P.C.
3226 28th Street, SE, Kentwood, Michigan 49512
Phone: (800) 785-1563 ◆ Fax: (800) 785-1563

Business Interests

TYPE: General and Limited Partnerships, Sole Proprietorships, privately-owned corporations, professional corporations, oil interests, farm, and ranch interests. **ADDITIONAL INFORMATION:** Give a description of the interests, who has the interest, your ownership in the interests, and the estimated value of the interests.

_____

_____

_____

_____

_____

_____

_____

Total   _____

Money Owed To You

TYPE: Mortgages or promissory notes payable **to you,** or other moneys owed to you.

Name of Debtor	Date of Note	Maturity Date	Owed to	Current Balance
_____	_____	_____	_____	_____
_____	_____	_____	_____	_____
_____	_____	_____	_____	_____
_____	_____	_____	_____	_____

Total   _____

Anticipated Inheritance, Gift, or Lawsuit Judgment

TYPE: Gifts or inheritances that you expect to receive at some time in the future; or moneys that you anticipate receiving through a judgment in a lawsuit. **Describe in appropriate detail.**

Description _____

_____

Total estimated value   _____

Other Assets

TYPE: Other property is any property that you have that does not fit into any listed category.

Type	Owner	Value
_____	_____	_____
_____	_____	_____
_____	_____	_____
_____	_____	_____
_____	_____	_____

Total   _____

Summary of Values

Assets	Amount*		
	Husband	Wife	Total Value
Real Property	_____	_____	_____
Furniture and Personal Effects	_____	_____	_____
Automobiles, Boats and RV's	_____	_____	_____
Bank and Savings Accounts	_____	_____	_____
Stocks and Bonds	_____	_____	_____
Life Insurance and Annuities	_____	_____	_____
Retirement Plans	_____	_____	_____
Business Interests	_____	_____	_____
Money owed to you	_____	_____	_____
Anticipated Inheritance, Etc.	_____	_____	_____
Other Assets	_____	_____	_____
Total Assets:	_____	_____	_____

*   *Joint Property values enter 1/2 in husband's column and 1/2 in wife's column.*

Law Office of James L. Moore, P.C.
3226 28th Street, SE, Kentwood, Michigan 49512
Phone: (800) 785-1563 ◆ Fax: (800) 785-1563

Appendix B

Reprinted with permission

A Guide to Picking the Right Trust

Set up the right way, trusts are a great way to protect assets. But beware of the pitfalls.

By Erin McCarthy, *Wall Street Journal*
Updated Nov. 9, 2014 4:46 p.m. ET

For many investors, trusts are an ideal way to keep portfolios safer for the long term.

The hard part is knowing what kind of trusts to set up and how to do it.

Trusts can protect assets from taxes and legal threats, and provide income for family and descendants for years to come. But if a trust isn't set up correctly, it can be ignored by the courts. Safeguards set up for family members may no longer exist, or planned tax savings may no longer be in effect.

Here's a look at several kinds of trusts, which ones work best for whom, and mistakes to avoid.

Irrevocable Life Insurance Trust

What It Is: This is used to buy life insurance on behalf of the person establishing the trust. The trust owns the insurance and pays the premium, and the benefits are paid into the trust. That way, the death benefit is isolated from estate tax, says Joan Crain, wealth strategist at BNY Mellon Wealth Management.

Life-insurance payouts can raise the risk that the insured's estate will be taxable. And if the estate is already taxable, the payouts make the taxes worse, says Robert Weiss, the global head of J.P. Morgan Private Bank's Advice Lab.

With a trust, the payouts won't increase the beneficiary's estate. The death benefit can be paid immediately or stay in trust for generations. The insured can put more than one policy into a single trust, or create multiple trusts for different beneficiaries. Policies in a trust also have some creditor protections.

Best for: The trusts are ideal for someone younger, who can obtain life insurance at affordable rates, and wants to protect any large insurance benefits from facing estate taxes.

Mistakes Often Made: Mr. Weiss says he has seen people set up a trust but never put the policy into it; others pay the premiums from their personal assets rather than from the trust. In such cases, those payments are not protected from any wealth-transfer taxes.

Granter Retained Annuity Trust

What It Is: Also known as GRATs, these trusts are typically short term, most commonly two to five years, and allow people to transfer their wealth to family members with little to no exposure to wealth-transfer taxes.

The granter places assets—such as cash, stocks or bonds—into the trust and each year receives an annuity payment. At the end of the trust's term, if the trust's assets have outperformed a "hurdle rate" set by the IRS—also known as the 7520 rate—those excess returns are distributed to the trust's beneficiaries or into another trust, free of gift and estate tax, J.P. Morgan says.

In recent years, low interest rates have resulted in an especially low hurdle rate, giving people more confidence their assets will outperform.

Best for: GRATs are ideal for granters who want to pass on assets to their own children while avoiding a hefty wealth-transfer tax. Through these short-term trusts, investors often try to take advantage of market volatility, placing assets in the trust that are expected to perform well in the next few years.

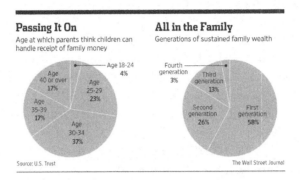

Passing It On
Age at which parents think children can handle receipt of family money

Age 18-24 4%
Age 40 or over 17%
Age 25-29 23%
Age 35-39 17%
Age 30-34 37%

All in the Family
Generations of sustained family wealth

Fourth generation 3%
Third generation 13%
Second generation 26%
First generation 58%

Source: U.S. Trust

The Wall Street Journal

Mistakes Often Made: One critical point: The granter must survive the term of the trust. If the granter dies before the trust reaches the end of its term, the trust collapses and the assets are returned to the granter's estate.

Dynasty Trust

What It Is: These trusts allow families to use wealth-transfer tax exemptions of up to $5.34 million per person to place assets into trust and let them grow untouched. "The idea there is that you're creating a family resource that's a pool for future generations," says Carol Kroch, managing director of wealth and philanthropic planning at Wilmington Trust Co.

Best for: They are for individuals thinking very, very long term. Then later, the trust can make tax-free distributions to the granter's children, grandchildren or future generations. The trust can specify whether beneficiaries will have access to its income or principal, and when. Such trusts can provide a great deal of tax savings.

Mistakes Often Made: Not all states allow dynasty trusts. Delaware, Pennsylvania, Rhode Island, Idaho and Louisiana are among the states that do.

Also, granters should use the trusts for assets they are confident will appreciate. If they use a wealth-transfer tax exemption to fund a trust with a stock that falls in value, the exemption ends up being wasted, Mr. Weiss says.

Qualified Personal Residence Trust

What It Is: A homeowner can place a residence in this trust—often a second home—to transfer the property later without paying full transfer taxes. The granter pays gift tax when the home goes into the trust, but on a reduced value of the house, since they reserve the right to live in it for the term of the trust, according to BNY Mellon Wealth Management. The value of the home for gift-tax purposes is the fair market value minus the present value of the granter's right to use it during the length of the trust (calculated using an IRS formula), J.P. Morgan says.

The trust lasts a certain number of years, and when it ends, the beneficiaries—often children—will own the residence. Any appreciation of the home since being placed in the trust is transferred to beneficiaries free of gift and estate tax. If the granter dies before the trust's term ends, the home is transferred back to the granter's estate.

Best for: People with vacation homes who know they want to give them away to their children or other family members down the line.

Mistakes Often Made: These trusts are most beneficial when interest rates are higher, since that results in a lower gift-tax value on the residence when it is placed in the trust.

Revocable Living Trust

What It Is: This is a trust created to hold and protect assets during an individual's lifetime. While it doesn't provide any tax savings, it does protect assets from probate. The individual creating the trust can also assign a successor trustee in the case of his/her death or incapacitation, which is a critical benefit, says Ms. Crain.

Best for: A revocable living trust makes sense for someone middle-aged or older who has money or investments that "they wouldn't want the court to take over if there's something that happens to them," Ms. Crain says. It also could be a good fit for someone seeking privacy, as a living trust is shielded from public scrutiny, rather than the estate being settled through probate, she adds.

Mistakes Often Made: Some investors don't put all the assets they should in the trust, so those assets are not protected from probate, Mr. Weiss says.

Charitable Remainder Trust

What It Is: Here, a granter puts assets into a trust and takes at least a 5% income interest, or assigns it to another beneficiary. What is left at the end of the trust's term goes to charity, and the granter receives an income-tax deduction for that amount, says Ms. Kroch of Wilmington Trust. The beneficiaries pay income taxes on the distributions.

Best for: These trusts are ideal for an investor who has assets that have already grown, since assets in the trust can be sold without incurring capital gains taxes, advisors say.

Mistakes Often Made: Ms. Kroch advises working with a trusted professional, as the rules are very detailed.

Ms. McCarthy is a reporter for The Wall Street Journal *in New York. Email* erin.mccarthy@wsj.com.

Appendix C

Price Versus Cost

Two couples were sitting in a meeting with our team of collaborative advisors. One couple was worth $35 million and the other was worth $2 million. The couple worth $2 million walked out of the meeting and said, "The price for all that brain power and experience is too rich for us." The couple worth $35 million left the meeting and said "We can't afford not to hire those people." It wasn't a matter of money; the people worth $2 million could definitely have afforded the help. It was their paradigm that kept them from getting the expertise they needed, and it was their paradigm that would keep them at $2 million and bar them from ever reaching $35 million.

Price and cost are not the same. Price is what you pay today. Cost equals the long-term effect of what you did or did not do. The price of any advice should always be weighed against the long-term costs, benefits, or overall savings. For example we once had a lady who did not want to do her Family Wealth Protection Planning™ because the price was too high, yet her inaction was going to cost her estate $10 million in estate and other taxes. Was the $15,000, or $100,000, or even $200,000 that she might have had to pay to get her wealth structured correctly too much to pay in order to save $10 million?

Should you be looking for a bargain when it comes down to setting and achieving your goals and/or managing your wealth? We hear it all the time: "My alma mater said they will set up my charitable trust and manage the money for free." "My son-in-law is a financial planner, and he said he'll do my estate plan and life insurance for a fraction of the cost others would charge." "My friend at church is an attorney who has a general practice and he said he could create an estate plan for me for less than half of what the firm who only does estate and business succession planning will charge." Have you ever heard these statements before? Our response to statements like these is, "Have you ever heard the phrase, *You get what you pay for*?" Price is only an issue when you fail to understand true value. Let me share a story I heard a long time ago that demonstrates this concept.

There was an elderly plant maintenance supervisor who made the hydro-electric plant where he worked hum like a well-oiled machine. For years, this intricately equipped monument to man's technological genius functioned so smoothly that hardly any members of the corporate board even knew there was a maintenance supervisor. Then came his retirement. Gold-watch time, the moment this quiet former janitor from the school of hard knocks stepped aside for a younger, credentialed professional engineer.

Shortly thereafter, there was a malfunction at the plant. Whatever it was, the entire operation was soon at a standstill. Neither the CEO, plant manager, nor the new young professional had the faintest idea of what to do about it. Every hour of down-time translated into $6,000 of lost revenue. Finally, someone thought to call the retired maintenance supervisor and ask him to come in and fix it. He obliged, donned his cap, and returned to his former workplace.

Within minutes of being briefed on the circumstances he walked around the plant for a while listening and looking and then walked over to a huge turbine, ran his hands along the side, and then tapped it at a certain place with a pipe wrench and everyone watched in amazement as the entire plant started back up. The old man left and the only trace of his presence was a hand written bill for his services. The total of the bill was $10,000, itemized as follows: (1) time to fix the problem, 10 minutes, charge $50; (2) knowledge and experience accumulated over a lifetime to know how to fix the problem—$9,550.

Was it worth it? Should he have worked up a sweat and made the repair seem more difficult for him in order to justify the bill? The CEO knew the true value of having the plant shut down and he knew the value of results. He happily paid the bill and had no trouble sleeping that night.

I don't mean to imply that you should pay an exorbitant fee for an acceptable result. Clearly, the fee should be in accord with what the market will bear. But what we need to understand is that what seems to be top-dollar fees can be, in reality, quite worth the price if not downright inexpensive when measured against the results, benefits, or savings they bring.

Expertise is the combination of knowledge and experience. Expertise is worth the price when it produces the desired results. Would you want your brain surgeon reading from a textbook during the operation? Do you want your attorney to charge you for research time when a more qualified attorney has implemented and defended the strategy or tactic successfully numerous times? Services you thought you were getting for less almost always end up costing you many times what a true specialist would have charged, because of a lack of experience, competence, or a hidden agenda. Price is only an issue in the absence of true value.

So, to the consumer I would say: Don't be cheap. If you're going to be a cheapskate, you're not going to get the best people to represent you. Do you deserve the best representation possible? It's unreasonable to say, "I want you to represent me. I want you to solve my problems. I want you to help me become fulfilled as a person and lead me to financial freedom so I can fulfill myself in every way," and then add, "Oh, by the way, I don't want to pay you what you're worth." If you're not willing to pay for the best, then you deserve to get discounted service. You're not going to get the same level of service and the same level of performance, but you're going to save a few bucks in the short term. If you're cheap, you're not going to get the expert representation you need and deserve.

In a world where nearly everything is being discounted or turned into a commodity, determining value is more difficult than ever before. If you surf the web you will find all kinds of free or discounted offers. "Free" software to help you do your own tax return is available by subscribing to certain magazines for a year. If you subscribe for two years, you can also receive an added bonus: software that will help you write your own living trust. And with a three-year subscription you will get a guide to allow you to do your own brain surgery! So called "free" investment advice is also everywhere. Do you really believe there is such a thing as excellent free advice? How can anything of great value actually be free? From time to time, you will come across some reasonably valuable free items or services, but nothing of great value ever comes easily or free. Often this is a cruel lesson of life. Let's hope you have already learned it.

Top-notch professionals utilize many different methods of billing or compensation. I believe the method used by the best or most excellent performers is a "value based" or "performance based" system.

In essence, value billing has very little to do with the time spent (i.e. hourly rate) and more to do with achieving the objective. Similar to the story of the retired plant maintenance supervisor, you are charged for the depth, breadth, and wisdom that come only through relevant and specific experience to deliver the desired result.

The best advice I can offer is this: In order to develop truly great outcomes, you must think and act in a win-win paradigm. To get what you want, you must help others get what they want. It must be fair for everyone, not just great for you. If you do not embrace this new paradigm of outcome-based value billing, then you must recognize that someone is losing. Anything less than a win-win situation equals a zero sum game in which only one party in the relationship receives true value.

Here's the most astounding part of this win-win paradigm: Great people produce great outcomes, and they cost less than people who quote or charge lower prices. Often the price of greatness is higher, but the overall cost is almost always less. I have learned that I get what I want when I make sure everyone involved sees the venture as personally rewarding monetarily, and enjoys both the work and the environment. Everyone then gets paid well and also has fun. Thus, everyone involved wins. What's more, they will be available and dedicated the next time I need their help.

Life is a team event. Success demands a great team comprised of all-stars. All-stars won't work if they aren't getting paid enough or if it isn't fun, because they don't have to work on unrewarding cases or with unpleasant or uncooperative people.

A few years ago I received a call from a financial advisor who had been referred to me by his firm's management. He demanded that I come to Alaska in February to meet with one of his "potential" clients. I politely declined. He complained to his manager, telling them that apparently I was arrogant because I had rejected this so-called "fantastic opportunity." "Don't you realize that this advisor is one of our largest producers?" they asked. "Most people would jump at the chance to work with him."

I gently explained that what was perceived as a "fantastic opportunity" by the advisor was not an attractive expenditure of the time, talent, and resources of the law firm at least at that point. For example, in our initial phone conversation the advisor had said, "I just prospected a guy who's worth over $50 million. I think I can drag him into a meeting with you." My response was, "I very much appreciate your confidence in our law firm. However, before we meet with someone it is important that we at least take a stab at deciding if we are going to be a fit, or not. Why don't we have an initial interview over the phone, or have you and your prospect attend one of our business owner webinars first and then decide if we all want to take the next step in our process." The advisor was shocked that I wasn't ready to hop on the next flight to Alaska (in February!) and astounded that the law firm had certain requirements that must be met before anyone expended time, energy, and money for a meeting.

This particular advisor was suffering from a type of business-culture clash. In his environment, someone would have to be nuts not to travel far and wide to meet face-to-face with someone worth $50 million. However, in our "value-based" culture at the Law Offices of James L. Moore, PC, we see it differently.

In order to make the most of everyone's time, talents, and resources, we have developed a system that enables us to meet only with truly interested and qualified potential clients. We have developed educational events for potential strategic planning partners and/or prospective clients. The investment of a couple of hours to attend a seminar or have a telephone or internet interactive conference is a small price to pay for a due diligence interview to see if they like our philosophy and planning process—or not. It also allows our firm to determine (a) whether we can provide value to them, and (b) whether it will be a pleasant and financially rewarding endeavor for everyone involved.

In the culture of our law firm, and also our supporting organization, The National Network of Estate Planning Attorneys, we are totally transparent. We have no hidden agenda, and we are not salespeople, because we receive a consistent flow of pre-qualified, motivated, collaborative referrals from both satisfied clients and other professional advisors within the tax and financial services industry. Our behavior is consistent with our mission to educate and empower people to act in their own best interests and thereby plan for, protect, and preserve their wealth and pass along their wisdom with their wealth.

Therefore, we provide books, videos, seminars, training, and consulting to help our collaborative professional planning partners and the people they serve to identify and achieve their goals. It is really quite simple.

The Law Offices of James L. Moore, P.C. seeks to:

- Help the client achieve a better vision of who they are and what they really want to accomplish.

- Educate both clients and their advisors.

- Empower clients, their families, their co-owners, and their advisors.

- Provide accurate macro and micro strategic plans which accurately describe and fulfill the client's desired outcomes.

- Facilitate outcomes in which everyone who should be or needs to be involved wins.

Some financial services firms have begun to see our system as a superior method of engaging in business. Neither the advisor in Alaska nor his manager appreciated our culture. They did not have a win-win, value-based paradigm. They live in a world where chasing clients is the norm. When you have a time tested and proven system you cannot deviate from it to satisfy those who won't even try to understand better methods.

The truth is that great people produce great outcomes. It is best if everyone has a financial stake in the desired outcome. Sales systems are unnecessary for this type of work. Client fulfillment systems and value-based, outcome-driven billing is the best way to deliver and receive great performance, and is the best win-win-win approach to doing business.

This creates a world where everyone wins and success is inevitable.

For more information about the Law Offices of James l. Moore visit www.lawofficesofjamesmoore.com/

CPSIA information can be obtained
at www.ICGtesting.com
Printed in the USA
FSOW04n1110231116
27752FS